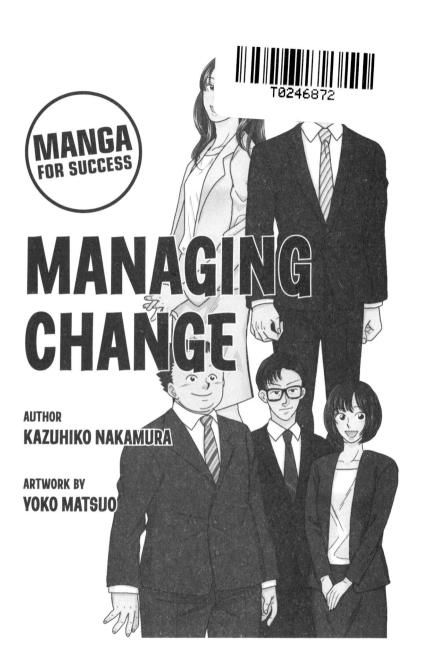

T0246872

MANGA
FOR SUCCESS

MANAGING
CHANGE

AUTHOR
KAZUHIKO NAKAMURA

ARTWORK BY
YOKO MATSUO

WILEY

For general information on our other products and services or for technical support, please contact our Customer Care Department within the United States at (800) 762-2974, outside the United States at (317) 572-3993 or fax (317) 572-4002.

Wiley also publishes its books in a variety of electronic formats. Some content that appears in print may not be available in electronic formats. For more information about Wiley products, visit our web site at www.wiley.com.

Library of Congress Cataloging-in-Publication Data is Available:
ISBN 9781394176229 (Paperback)
ISBN 9781394176236 (ePub)
ISBN 9781394176243 (ePDF)

Cover Design: JMA Management Center Inc.
Cover Images: JMA Management Center Inc.
© ShEd Artworks/Shutterstock

SKY1004729_031023

Contents

Part 2	The Core Team as an Agent of Change

Part 3	From Individual Work to Cooperation

Part 5	Deepening and Expansion throughout the Organization as a Whole

Epilogue

Introduction

You may have picked up this book because things aren't going very well at work or it could be that you just want to improve your current workplace or organization. There are probably also a lot of you who just can't seem to figure out what to do to improve things at work or in your organization.

Organization Development can give you hints and ideas on what steps you can take in order to achieve these goals.

The concept of Organization Development, however, isn't just one single method that you can immediately apply. It's a label of sorts that's used to refer to a collection of various techniques and ideas. You can think of this like how the term "Ball games" is an umbrella term for many different sports that use a ball such as baseball, soccer, and table tennis, among many others.

Although the concept of "Organization Development" evolved during the 1930s, it only began gaining popularity in Japan in 2015 or so. In the United States, it began to take off in the 1960s. Before that, it was more common to use the term "Workplace Stimulation" or "Organization Stimulation" when dealing with office or organization improvement (and these terms are still used now).

As such, you can take all these three terms to mean the same thing.

Organization Development is a term adopted from the global stage. It was first coined in the United States in 1958, and it developed and spread mainly in America and Europe to include a wide array of theories and techniques. Now, an increasing number of Japanese companies choose to have a specialized department dedicated to Organization Development that is focused on handling workplace-related and organizational improvements.

More and more Japanese companies are engaging in Organization Development, but what is causing this movement? I believe it's because **it's becoming harder for people in an office or organization to rely on, cooperate, and actively work with each other.**

There are many reasons behind this. The following are three factors that could be causing the above-mentioned workplace difficulties.

(1) The Rise of Individual Work

Often, the manager divides the work and assigns a task to each person and who will then work on their task alone (other people in the workplace do not know what other people are working on). With increasing workload and the work-style reform being implemented, there are more situations where employees have to efficiently complete the work assigned to them by themselves. Since there is no one around to support them, employees suffer from higher stress levels, which could even lead to mental health issues.

(2) Increasing Diversity in the Workplace

When people of varying age, gender, disability (if any), nationality, and employment status work together in the same place, the differences in their language, way of thinking, methods, and work values may make it harder to relate and cooperate with each other. Having a diverse set of people in a team offers the advantage of more easily coming up with new ideas, but in order to do that, the team members will first have to overcome their differences.

(3) Decreasing Discussion Time as an Effect of Optimization and Work-style Reform

There are three things needed for multiple people to be able to work together and cooperate with each other:

① First, they need to work as a team. ② They will also need to share their work methods with each other and come up with a consensus on how to proceed. ③ Each member will need to understand how they're affecting the people around them and vice versa. However, nowadays, there is usually less time for communication in the workplace (or communication is mostly done through email), so this communication tends to be about work and work alone. With limited communication, there tend to be mismatches in everyone's work methods, intentions, and thoughts. This gives rise to conflicts and makes cooperation more difficult.

With remote work becoming more common, cooperation will probably become even more difficult from here on.

In short, there are many factors in our current work arrangements that make it harder for people in an office or organization to rely on, cooperate, and actively work with each other. You may even say that **the difficulty of workplace stimulation and teamwork management is at an all-time high.**

Due to these circumstances, there is a focus on Organization Development as a way of **approaching the challenge of increasing cooperation and teamwork in order to make a workplace or organization a more lively place to work in.**

As mentioned earlier, Organization Development is a framework that includes various theories and techniques. For this book, we won't be focusing on explaining and breaking down a single technique or method. In order to understand the basics of Organization Development, we will be going through its basic methods. **We will look at what approaches and attitudes are important when it comes to Organization Development and how to think about discussion and change in general.**

As you read this book, you will see how the main characters like the manager and Sakigake-san, among others, change as the story goes on. I hope that this will give you some insight on the various circumstances people face, the different ways of discussing matters, and the changes in how people relate to each other. Hopefully, this will also give you ideas on how to proceed with your own Organization Development.

Kazuhiko Nakamura

Problems Keep Happening Yet the Workplace Stays the Same

STORY 1
THE UNCHANGING WORKPLACE

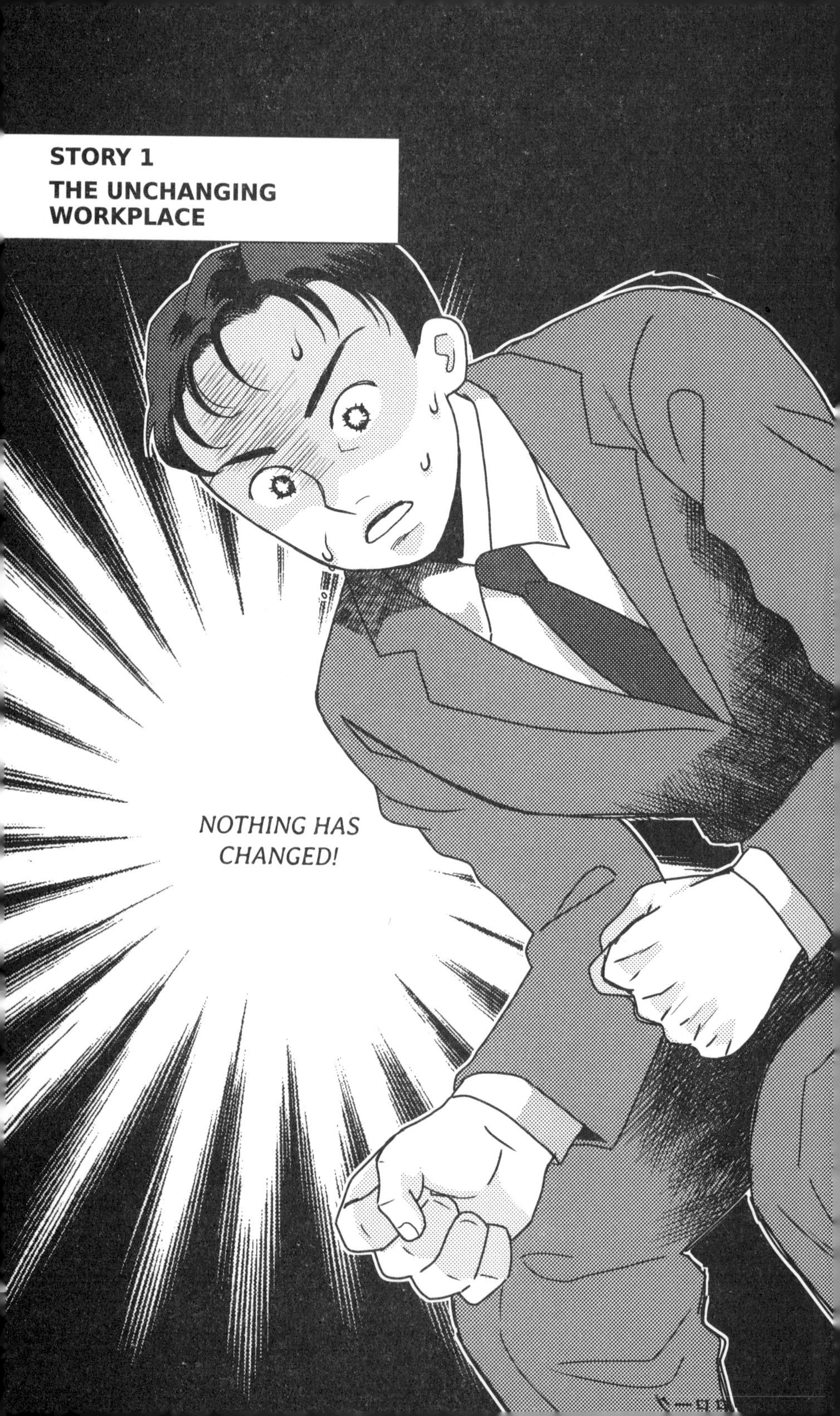
NOTHING HAS CHANGED!

THIS IS IMPOSSIBLE. NOTHING CHANGES NO MATTER WHAT I DO.

I'M AT MY WITS' END.

HOW DID WE EVEN GET HERE?

A FEW MON- THS AGO.

TAIGA MOTOR COM- PANY HEAD OFFICE.

STORE MANAG- ER?

HUMAN RESOURC DEPARTMENT

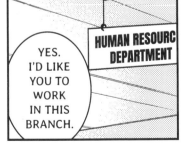

YES. I'D LIKE YOU TO WORK IN THIS BRANCH.

THIS BRANCH HAS A GOOD TRACK RECORD THOUGH, DOESN'T IT?

STORE MANAGER / SALES

CHUJI SAKIGAKE

YES. THEY SHOW GOOD NUMBERS, BUT THEY ALSO HAVE A HIGHER RATE OF LEAVES AND RESIGNATIONS THAN OTHER BRANCHES.

SO IT'S A SOME-WHAT ODD BRANCH.

IF THE SITUATION IS LEFT AS IT IS, IT'S LIKELY THAT THEIR SALES WILL ALSO FALL EVENTUALLY.

I SEE WHAT YOU MEAN.

SO YOU WANT ME TO GO TO THIS BRANCH AND REMEDY THE PROBLEM, CORRECT?

YES. I BELIEVE YOU HAVE WHAT IT TAKES TO DO THIS.

CAR DEALERS HAVE TO DEAL WITH A LOT OF THINGS AT WORK.

ASIDE FROM CAR SALES ITSELF...

THEY HAVE TO KEEP UP WITH ALL THESE NUMBERS EVERY DAY, NO, EVERY HOUR, NO, EVERY MINUTE.

...THEY ALSO HAVE TO DEAL WITH IN- SPECTIONS AND IN- SURANCE SALES AND RENEWAL.

GAAAH!

IT'S A STORE MANAGER'S JOB TO OVERSEE ALL OF THESE THINGS. THAT IS WHY...

...THEIR ABILITY IS USUALLY DIRECTLY REFLECTED IN THE STORE'S SALES.

MY NAME IS SAKIGAKE. I'M GOING TO BE YOUR NEW STORE MANAGER STARTING TODAY.

I LOOK FORWARD TO WORK- ING WITH ALL OF YOU.

19

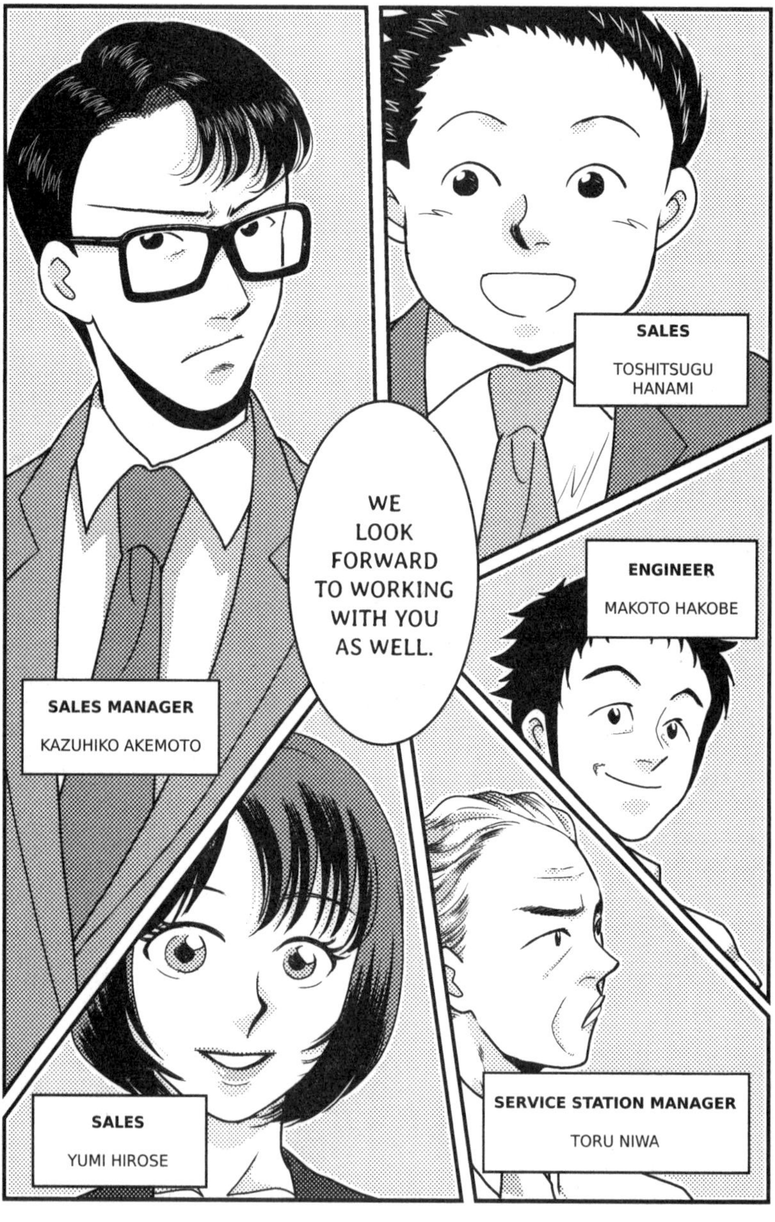
SALES MANAGER
KAZUHIKO AKEMOTO
SALES
TOSHITSUGU HANAMI
WE LOOK FORWARD TO WORKING WITH YOU AS WELL.
ENGINEER
MAKOTO HAKOBE
SALES
YUMI HIROSE
SERVICE STATION MANAGER
TORU NIWA

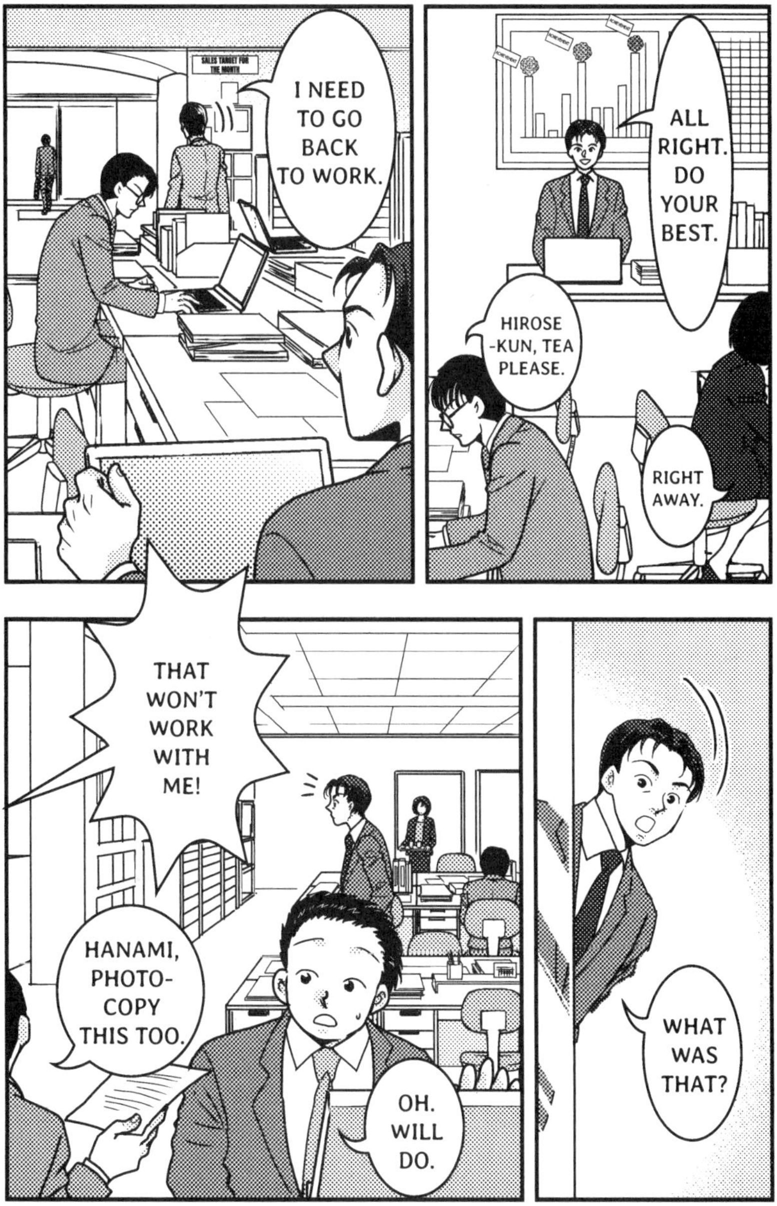
SALES TARGET FOR THE MONTH
I NEED TO GO BACK TO WORK.
ALL RIGHT. DO YOUR BEST.
HIROSE -KUN, TEA PLEASE.
RIGHT AWAY.
THAT WON'T WORK WITH ME!
HANAMI, PHOTO- COPY THIS TOO.
OH. WILL DO.
WHAT WAS THAT?

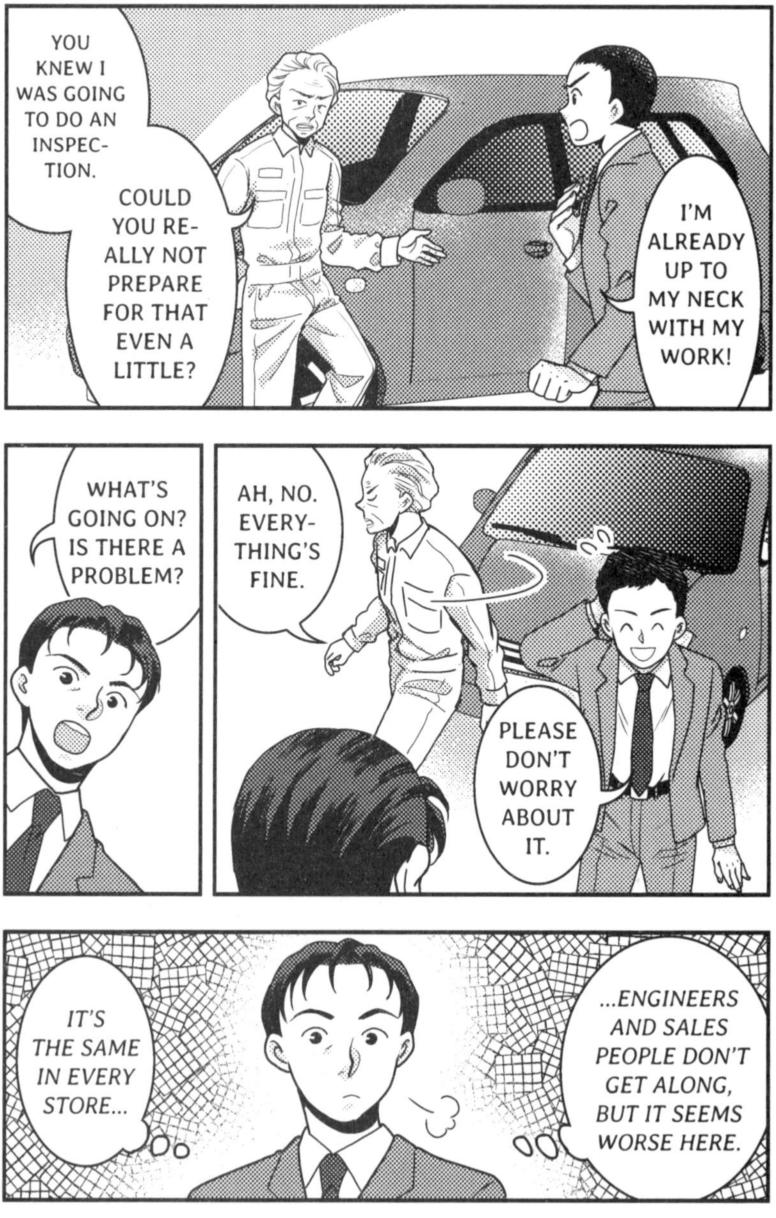
YOU KNEW I WAS GOING TO DO AN INSPEC- TION.
COULD YOU RE- ALLY NOT PREPARE FOR THAT EVEN A LITTLE?
I'M ALREADY UP TO MY NECK WITH MY WORK!
WHAT'S GOING ON? IS THERE A PROBLEM?
AH, NO. EVERY- THING'S FINE.
PLEASE DON'T WORRY ABOUT IT.
IT'S THE SAME IN EVERY STORE...
...ENGINEERS AND SALES PEOPLE DON'T GET ALONG, BUT IT SEEMS WORSE HERE.

I'M BACK.

WEL-COME BACK.

...

CLATTER

THE EM-PLOYEES DON'T TALK TO EACH OTHER AT ALL.

A BIT OF A CHILLY ATMO-SPHERE HERE.

CLACK

CLACK

...

...

WHIRR WELCOME

GASP

OH! THAT'S IT!

AH, YOU PROBABLY WOULDN'T KNOW ABOUT THAT, COULD YOU CALL SOMEBODY ELSE FOR ME?

THE PROBLEM IS THAT EVERYONE'S JUST CONCERNED WITH THEIR OWN WORK! NO ONE INTERACTS, AND THERE'S NO COOPERATIVE ENERGY AT ALL!

THINGS SHOULD GET BETTER IF THE WORKERS INTERACTED MORE AND THE OFFICE BECOMES LIVELIER!

NOW THAT I KNOW THE PROBLEM, I CAN LOOK FOR BOOKS ON THE MATTER.

CLICK CLACK

ALL RIGHT! DOWN-LOADS DONE.

I'LL READ THROUGH THESE TO-NIGHT AND FORMULATE A PLAN.

THE NEXT DAY.

TAIGA MOTOR COMPANY STORE

TAIGA

STARTING TODAY, WE'LL BE HOLDING DAILY MEETINGS INSTEAD OF MONTHLY ONES.

LET'S TRY TO BE MORE ACTIVE IN SHARING IDEAS WITH ONE ANOTHER.

...

...

WHAT DO YOU THINK, AKEMOTO-SAN?

I DON'T MIND AS LONG AS THE NUMBERS GO UP.

HANAMI-KUN?

I- I DON'T MIND EITHER.

I SEE ...

THE RESPONSES AREN'T VERY PROMISING. I GUESS I'LL TRY SOMETHING ELSE.

A FEW DAYS LATER.

TODAY, I'D LIKE ALL OF US TO REVISIT OUR MEDIUM-TERM BUSINESS PLAN TOGETHER.

PLEASE WRITE DOWN YOUR VISION FOR THE NEXT TWO TO THREE YEARS ON THIS SHEET.

CHILL

O-OH, RIGHT. YAMAZAKI-KUN'S ON LEAVE STARTING THIS WEEK.

WHAT SHOULD WE DO WITH HIS WORK?

THESE ARE YAMAZAKI'S ASSIGNMENTS.

THE TWO OF YOU CAN TAKE ONE EACH.

HUH?!

OKAY.

UNDERSTOOD.

THEY'RE BEING GIVEN MORE WORK. WHY AREN'T THEY COMPLAINING?!

WHY DOESN'T ANYONE TRY TO COMMUNICATE EVEN A LITTLE?!

COULD IT BE THAT THIS PLACE IS DOOMED?

WILL NOTHING CHANGE NO MATTER WHAT I DO?

CHILL

HEY.

HEY, SAKI-GAKE!

ORGANIZATION DEVELOPMENT

PUB

JOLT

O-OH.

SORRY, YOU WERE SAYING?

...

TH-THAT'S RIGHT. I WANTED TO TALK TO SOMEONE...

WAIT, SO YOU WEREN'T LISTENING?

...SO I INVITED A FORMER COLLEAGUE FROM MAN-AGEMENT PLANNING...

...TO COME HAVE A DRINK WITH ME.

WELL, I HEARD YOU WERE ASSIGNED TO TAKE CARE OF A PROBLEMATIC BRANCH.

I GUESS YOU'RE HAVING A HARD TIME, HUH?

Y-YEAH.

IT'S LIKE THERE'S NO RE-SPONSE NO MAT-TER WHAT I DO.

28

I SEE. HOW'S THE NUMBERS?

SLOWLY DROPPING.

SLOWLY'S PROBABLY EVEN WORSE.

THAT'S WHY I'VE BEEN TRYING...

...TO THINK OF ANYTHING THAT MIGHT HELP US BREAK OUT FROM THIS STALEMATE.

HMM...

OH, WAIT.

HAVE YOU CONSULTED THE ORGANIZATION DEVELOPMENT TEAM FROM HR YET?

!

TH-THAT'S RIGHT! I FORGOT ABOUT THEM!

THE ORGANIZATION DEVELOPMENT TEAM...

GOOD MORNING.

...

SILENCE...

CLICK CLACK

I DON'T KNOW THE DETAILS, BUT I BELIEVE THEY'RE SUPPOSED TO BE A TEAM THAT HELPS WITH IMPROVING EMPLOYEE RELATIONS IN THE COMPANY.

THEIR ADDRESS SHOULD BE IN THE COMPANY NETWORK.

CLICK CLACK

THAT'S WHY UP UNTIL RECENTLY, I NEVER THOUGHT I'D HAVE ANYTHING TO DO WITH THEM.

FOR ANY CONSULTATIONS REGARDING WORKPLACE CONDITIONS, YOU CAN REACH US AT THE ADDRESS BELOW.

HUMAN RESOURCES ORGANIZATION DEVELOPMENT TEAM

AAA@MAIL.NE.JP

HERE IT IS.

"MY NAME IS SAKIGAKE, AND I'M THE STORE MANAGER AT THE MIDORIOKA BRANCH. I'D LIKE TO CONSULT YOU ABOUT OUR CURRENT WORKPLACE CONDITIONS. WOULD YOU BE AVAILABLE FOR A MEETING REGARDING THIS? PLEASE LET ME KNOW."

AND SENT.

IF THIS STILL DOESN'T WORK, I REALLY DON'T KNOW WHAT TO DO ANYMORE.

CLACK

BEEP

1 NEW MAIL

AH.

A FEW DAYS LATER.

TAIGA MOTOR COMPANY HEAD OFFICE.

MEETING ROOM 003

IN USE

I'M SORRY TO HAVE KEPT YOU WAITING.

Y-YES!

YOU'RE SAKIGAKE-SAN, AM I CORRECT?

!

The branch Sakigake was assigned to as store manager was performing well, but it also had the following problems:

- There is no conversation between the employees, and they don't try to communicate with one another.
- There's no energy in the workplace atmosphere.
- The rate of people going on leave and resigning is high.
- There's conflict between the sales people and the engineers.

Sakigake first tries to solve the problem in the sales department by looking up solutions on the Internet. He then introduced daily morning meetings and held a workshop to have the employees come up with their own individual vision based on the company's medium-term business plan. However, neither of these work, and both of these efforts couldn't even draw a response from the employees.

There are probably a lot of workplaces similar to the one in the story. Lack of communication, lack of energy, and conflict between employees are problems you will likely find in lots of offices. A lot of surveys show that poor relationships with coworkers is one of the top reasons people have for quitting their job. There is a desire to resolve conflicts and improve relationships between employees in the workplace, **but the reality is that when typical solutions are implemented, they often don't work well.**

In this section, we'll tackle how to think about conflicts between people in the workplace or an organization and think about why common solutions don't work to resolve these conflicts.

Just like in the manga, many workplaces struggle with where and how to start solving their problems.

Just like in the manga, many workplaces struggle with where and how to start solving their problems.

The Human Side of Workplaces and Organizations

◆ The Hard and Soft Sides of an Organization

Every workplace and organization has an official hard side and an unofficial soft side. In organization psychology, this is referred to as the official and unofficial organization, or as the organization's hard and soft structures.

The hard side consists of things that are decided and stipulated, such as the organization's structure (departments and divisions), the company strategy and medium-term business plan, the employee grade system, the personnel system, job descriptions, work procedures that have been compiled into manuals, IT systems, performance rewards, etc. These types of information can be found in documentation or looked up in the company intranet and are easily visible to everyone. They're written down, so as long as someone reads them, there won't be any big discrepancies in how people understand them. (Of course, it's possible that people will have different interpretations and attach different meanings to these.)

On the other hand, the soft side consists of what goes on in people's minds and their behaviors. These include communication conditions, decision-making processes, trust, cooperation, competition, power balance and relationships, the state of leadership, sharing and instillment of goals and strategies, motivations and feelings, assumptions and preconceptions, energy and atmosphere, culture and traditions, etc. These are all things that go on within or between individuals. The soft side is also known as the human side of organizations.

Figure 1-1 The Hard and Soft Sides of Organizations	
Hard Side	Soft Side
Organization structure, strategy, medium-term business plan, personnel system, manual, IT system, performance rewards, etc.	Communication conditions, decision-making processes, relationships between people, motivations, assumptions, atmosphere, culture and traditions, etc.

Things that fall under the human side are usually unwritten and aren't easily visible to everyone. People will usually have different views and understandings of these types of things. For instance, some employees could think that communication within the office is bad while others could think that it's great even though they work in the same place. In this sense, not all of the employees in a workplace will necessarily see the situation in the same way, and it could be that only a portion will feel that there's a problem in the human side of the organization. This is exactly what the soft side (human side) of an organization is—the side that's not easily visible and seen differently by different people.

◆ Why Managing the Human Side Is Important

As shown in Figure 1-2, the hard and soft sides of a workplace or organization can be likened to an iceberg. The portion of the iceberg that's above the water is the hard side while the portion that's under the water is the soft side, which is the human side. Just as the iceberg portion above the water is very visible, the hard side of an organization is also easy to see. On the other hand, the portion below the water, which represents the human side (this goes on within people's minds, so not everything is verbalized) is hidden away from sight.

Shown in Figure 1-2 are factors under these two sides at the individual, workplace, and organization levels.

To improve the performance of their workplaces and teams, managers set official targets and roles, clearly define work procedures, and evaluate their subordinates according to set rules. However, good management of the hard side doesn't guarantee a good performance. Performance is also affected by factors that fall under the human side such as how motivating or convincing the work targets are and

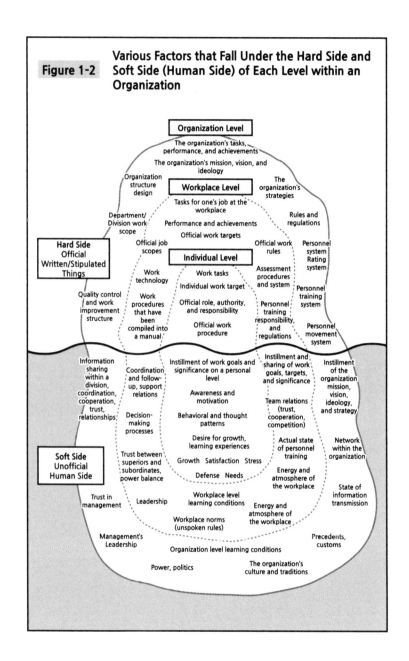

Figure 1-2 Various Factors that Fall Under the Hard Side and Soft Side (Human Side) of Each Level within an Organization

Organization Level
The organization's tasks, performance, and achievements
The organization's mission, vision, and ideology

Organization structure design

Workplace Level
Tasks for one's job at the workplace
Performance and achievements
Official work targets

The organization's strategies

Rules and regulations

Department/ Division work scope

Hard Side
Official
Written/Stipulated
Things

Official job scopes

Individual Level
Work tasks
Individual work target
Official role, authority, and responsibility
Official work procedure

Official work rules

Assessment procedures and system

Personnel training responsibility, and regulations

Personnel system
Rating system

Personnel training system

Personnel movement system

Quality control and work improvement structure

Work technology

Work procedures that have been compiled into a manual

Information sharing within a division, coordination, cooperation, trust, relationships

Coordination and follow-up, support relations

Decision-making processes

Instillment of work goals and significance on a personal level

Awareness and motivation

Behavioral and thought patterns

Desire for growth, learning experiences

Instillment and sharing of work goals, targets, and significance

Team relations (trust, cooperation, competition)

Instillment of the organization mission, vision, ideology, and strategy

Network within the organization

Soft Side
Unofficial
Human Side

Trust between superiors and subordinates, power balance

Growth Satisfaction Stress

Defense Needs

Actual state of personnel training

Energy and atmosphere of the workplace

State of information transmission

Trust in management

Leadership

Workplace level learning conditions

Workplace norms (unspoken rules)

Energy and atmosphere of the workplace

Management's Leadership

Organization level learning conditions

Power, politics

The organization's culture and traditions

Precedents, customs

cooperation and support relations within the workplace. If a problem in the human side of the workplace is left unnoticed and unsolved, it can become a hindrance to improving performance. On top of that, it can also lead to mental health issues, which can increase the frequency of leaves and resignations. This means that **management of the human side of a workplace is a crucial task for a manager.**

Many people study techniques to deal with human side problems to make the workplace more lively through coaching, one-on-one discussions, and meeting facilitation. Learning these techniques can be useful, but there's also a pitfall (just as in the story, the store manager Sakigake implemented the techniques he learned on the Internet, but they didn't work).

So **why is it that directly applying standard techniques to solve human side problems in an organization or workplace doesn't work very well?** We'll look at the reasons for this in the following pages.

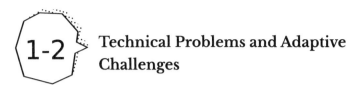

1-2 Technical Problems and Adaptive Challenges

◆ There Are Two Sides to a Problem

Ronald Heifetz, a researcher who studies leadership, proposed that problems in the world can be classified into **technical problems** and **adaptive challenges.**

A simple explanation of technical problems and adaptive challenges can be found in Figure 1-3.

Technical problems include equipment and machine failure, mechanical troubles in production, needs for technique improvement, and lack of individual skill. For mechanical equipment and machine failures, finding the cause and applying standard solutions is enough to solve the problem. Skill-related problems include being unable to use certain software and a lack of communication and presentation skills. These types of problems can be solved by acquiring the skill in question.

On the other hand, adaptive challenges are problems that require the people involved to adapt to the current situation. When dealing with these problems, there is

Figure 1-3   Technical Problems and Adaptive Challenges

Technical Problems	Adaptive Challenges
The problem is clearly defined (you can identify the problem)	The problem is not clearly defined (situation needs to be studied to find the problem)
The solution is known	Solutions for challenges that require adaptation aren't known
Possible to solve with standard solutions or approaches	There is no existing solution (cannot be solved with existing mindsets)
Possible to solve by using appropriate knowledge and techniques	There is a need to change established ways of thinking and behavior
Can be solved by someone who has specialized knowledge and skills	Research and study with the people involved is needed
The problem is found outside the person(s) concerned	The person(s) concerned is (are) part of the problem (the thought and behavior patterns of the person influence the problem)

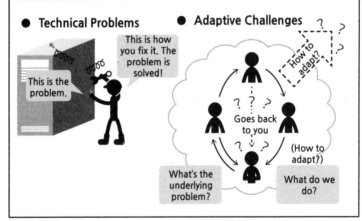

a need to change one's thought patterns and behavior. Adaptation will be necessary for both external and internal (within the workplace) matters. For these challenges, you cannot just apply existing, standard solutions as they are. The people concerned will have to study the problem in terms of themselves (how they understand the problem and their assumptions), discuss what to do, and come up with a solution together while also learning things individually.

◆ Common Leader and Manager Mistakes

An example that Heifetz presented was an old person driving a car at night and damaging it. Fixing the car is a technical problem. However, the old person will also have to face the reality of not being able to drive at night anymore. If he decides to stop driving, he can no longer drive by himself to a restaurant at night. Driving was his pride, and if he stops, he will feel like he has lost a part of his identity. This is an example of an adaptive challenge.

Let's think of an example applicable to a Japanese or even a Western workplace. Let's say that there's a team assigned to repair and do maintenance on a machine in the manufacturing line. Fixing this machine when it malfunctions is a technical problem. On the other hand, let's say that the team leader had to retire due to old age but remained in the team as a member. Another team member then moves up to become the new team leader. This new team leader will have to face the challenge of leading a team with a member who's more experienced and whose words carry more weight. Learning how to unite this team and demonstrate your own leadership in this kind of situation is an adaptive challenge.

Let's also consider the challenge of holding online meetings with people overseas. Making the sound and video quality as high as possible for these meetings is a technical problem. At the same time, learning how to communicate, come to agreements, and understand each other as a team with members from different cultures is an adaptive challenge.

What about the problem in the manga's story? Do you think they're facing a technical problem or an adaptive challenge?

1-3　Adaptive Challenges and Organization Development

◆ Problems in the Human Side Include Adaptive Challenges

Human problems in workplaces and organizations usually aren't caused by one single thing or person. Instead, they're usually the result of a complex tangle of many different factors. These problems are also harder to see, and you can say that these situations are usually uncharted territory.

In short, problems on the human side of organizations and workplaces usually include adaptive challenges.

Let's take a person who has a hard time sharing their thoughts and opinions in the workplace. If the problem is only this person's communication skills, then this can be tackled as a technical problem by learning how to communicate. It's also possible that there isn't a lot of time and opportunity for communication in the workplace, and this situation can be resolved as a technical problem by holding regular meetings.

However, in the story, the human problem in their branch was the lack of response to the store manager's directions and the lack of energy and communication between employees. The people involved have the necessary skills to communicate and respond, yet the trouble is still there. This type of problem has to do with the employees' thoughts and behaviors, and it includes more complex **adaptive challenges.**

The store manager, Sakigake, tried to solve this problem by directly applying standard techniques. As shown in the story, these types of problems usually cannot be resolved in this manner.

The reality is that it's hard to get the results you expect when you just directly apply standard techniques to human problems in an organization or workplace. In contrast to this kind of approach (the solutions Sakigake tried to apply), **Organization Development** tackles these types of challenges by studying the problem together as a group and breaking down the situation in order to formulate a strategy and implement it together.

Part 1

What Is Organization Development?

STORY 2
MEETING A SUPPORTER OF ORGANIZATION DEVELOPMENT

IT'S NICE TO MEET YOU. I'M NANAKO MIZUSHINA FROM THE ORGANIZATION DEVELOPMENT TEAM.

IT'S NICE TO MEET YOU AS WELL. I'M CHUJI SAKIGAKE, STORE MANAGER OF THE MIDORIOKA BRANCH.

BOW

THANK YOU FOR COMING TO MEET ME TODAY.

YOU'RE HERE TO DISCUSS HOW TO HELP IMPROVE YOUR BRANCH, RIGHT?

CLATTER

CLATTER

YES.

BEFORE WE BEGIN, I'D LIKE TO EXPLAIN EXACTLY WHAT OUR TEAM DOES.

HOW MUCH DO YOU KNOW ABOUT ORGANIZATION DEVELOPMENT?

I HAVE A GENERAL IDEA OF WHAT YOUR TEAM DOES...

...BUT THIS IS MY FIRST TIME CONTACTING YOU AND REQUESTING YOUR SERVICES.

I SEE.

WELL, THE TERM "ORGANIZATION DEVELOPMENT"...

...DOESN'T ACTUALLY HAVE A SINGLE, RIGID DEFINITION.

PEOPLE OFTEN HAVE A VERY VAGUE IMPRESSION OF WHAT IT IS.

47

TO PUT IT SIMPLY, ORGANIZATION DEVELOPMENT INVOLVES HAVING SELECTED INDIVIDUALS FACILITATE DISCUSSION TO UNDERSTAND THEIR SITUATION, MAKE A PLAN, AND EXECUTE IT IN ORDER TO IMPROVE THEIR WORKPLACE OR ORGANIZATION.

THE PEOPLE INVOLVED DISCUSS TO UNDERSTAND THEIR SITUATION...

IT DOESN'T REFER TO A SINGLE METHOD THOUGH. THE PROCESS TAKES INTO ACCOUNT THE HUMAN SIDE OF ORGANIZATIONS AND WORKPLACES AND REFERS TO A SET OF IDEAS AND TECHNIQUES FOR APPROACHING IT.

THE HUMAN SIDE REFERS TO FACTORS SUCH AS PEOPLE'S FEELINGS, MOTIVATIONS, COMMUNICATION, TRUST, COOPERATION, AND OTHER SUCH THINGS THAT ARE DIFFICULT TO SEE.

WELL THEN, CAN YOU TELL ME ABOUT YOUR STORE'S SITUATION IN DETAIL?

LET'S SEE. FIRST OF ALL, THERE'S NO MOTIVATION AT ALL IN THE WORKPLACE ...

I SEE. WELL, JUDGING BY YOUR SITUATION...

...WE WANT TO BRING THESE PREVIOUSLY IGNORED PROBLEMS TO LIGHT. HOW ABOUT WE TRY DIAGNOSIS ORGANIZATION DEVELOPMENT?

DIAGNOSIS?

BASICALLY, DIAGNOSIS ORGANIZATION DEVELOPMENT INVOLVES...

...GATHERING AND ANALYZING DATA TO BRING ATTENTION TO THE ISSUES AND HAVING A SERIOUS DISCUSSION ABOUT THE RESULTS.

S-SERIOUS?!

OH. IT MEANS GIVING FEEDBACK. DOES THAT MAKE IT CLEARER?

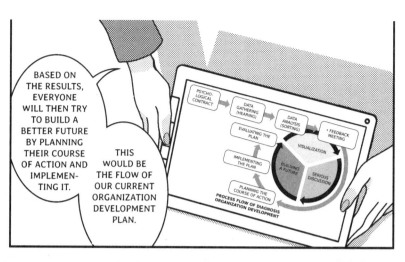

BASED ON THE RESULTS, EVERYONE WILL THEN TRY TO BUILD A BETTER FUTURE BY PLANNING THEIR COURSE OF ACTION AND IMPLEMENTING IT.

THIS WOULD BE THE FLOW OF OUR CURRENT ORGANIZATION DEVELOPMENT PLAN.

VISUALIZATION... SERIOUS DISCUSSION... FUTURE BUILDING...

THIS IS THE FIRST TIME I'VE SEEN A PROCESS LIKE THIS. CAN WE REALLY DO THIS?

BUT MAYBE THIS'LL WORK!

I'LL DO IT! I LOOK FORWARD TO WORKING WITH YOU, THEN!

I LOOK FORWARD TO WORKING WITH YOU AS WELL.

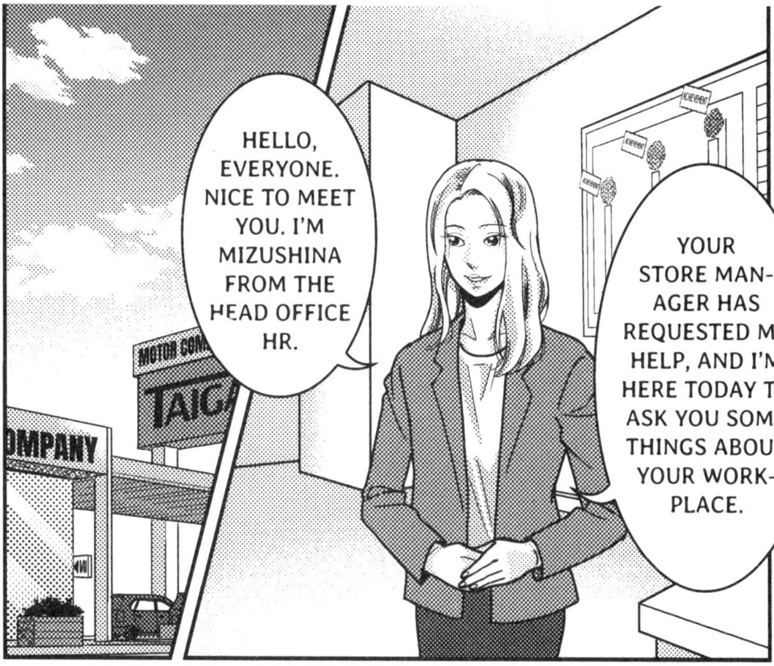
MOTOR COM
TAIG
OMPANY
HELLO, EVERYONE. NICE TO MEET YOU. I'M MIZUSHINA FROM THE HEAD OFFICE HR.
YOUR STORE MANAGER HAS REQUESTED MY HELP, AND I'M HERE TODAY TO ASK YOU SOME THINGS ABOUT YOUR WORKPLACE.

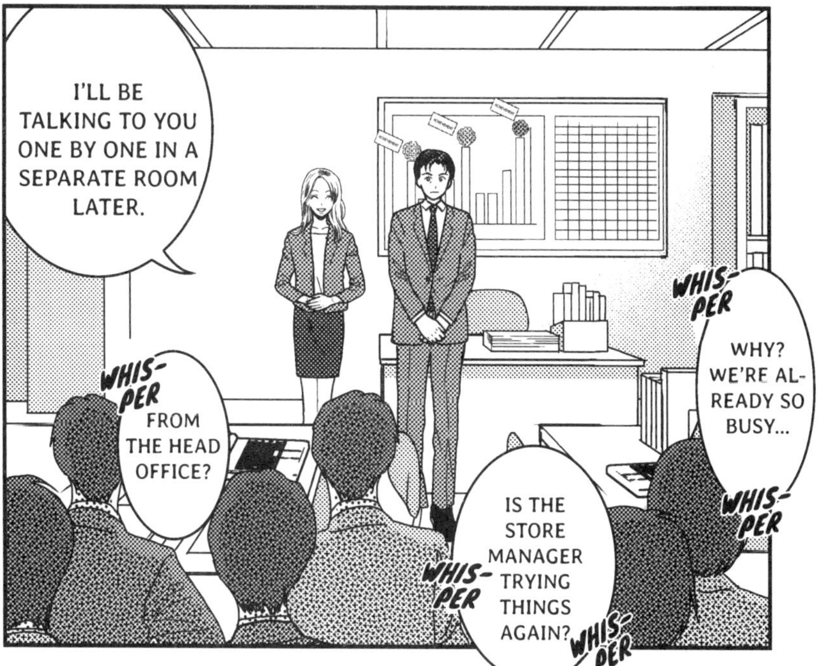
I'LL BE TALKING TO YOU ONE BY ONE IN A SEPARATE ROOM LATER.
WHIS-PER
WHY? WE'RE ALREADY SO BUSY...
WHIS-PER
FROM THE HEAD OFFICE?
WHIS-PER
IS THE STORE MANAGER TRYING THINGS AGAIN?
WHIS-PER
WHIS-PER

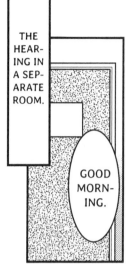

THE HEARING IN A SEPARATE ROOM.

GOOD MORNING.

THANK YOU FOR TAKING TIME OUT OF YOUR BUSY DAY TO DO THIS.

YOUR ANSWERS HERE WILL BE SHARED WITH EVERYONE LATER, BUT EVERYTHING WILL BE ANONYMOUS.

COULD YOU TELL ME WHAT YOU THINK ABOUT THIS BRANCH?

ANYTHING WILL DO, SO PLEASE DON'T HESITATE TO SHARE YOUR THOUGHTS.

AH...

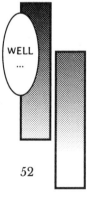

WELL...

A FEW DAYS LATER. TAIGA MOTOR COMPANY HEAD OFFICE.

I'VE COMPILED THE RESULTS OF OUR HEARING FROM A FEW DAYS AGO.

HOW DID EVERYONE RESPOND?

THEY HAD A LOT TO SAY.

SO THEY SHARED THEIR OPIN-IONS WITH YOU...

FROM THEIR PERSPECTIVE, SINCE I'M NOT PART OF THE COMPANY...

...AND SINCE THEY WERE PROMISED ANONYMITY, IT WAS EASY FOR THEM TO BE HONEST.

HERE ARE THE RESULTS OF THE HEAR-ING.

CLICK

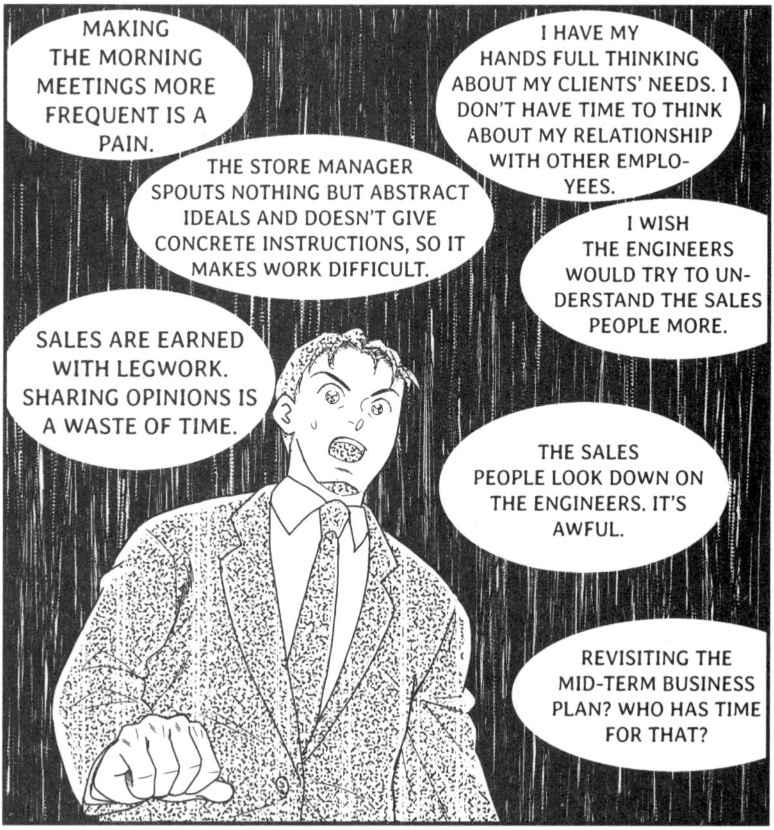
MAKING THE MORNING MEETINGS MORE FREQUENT IS A PAIN.
I HAVE MY HANDS FULL THINKING ABOUT MY CLIENTS' NEEDS. I DON'T HAVE TIME TO THINK ABOUT MY RELATIONSHIP WITH OTHER EMPLO-YEES.
THE STORE MANAGER SPOUTS NOTHING BUT ABSTRACT IDEALS AND DOESN'T GIVE CONCRETE INSTRUCTIONS, SO IT MAKES WORK DIFFICULT.
I WISH THE ENGINEERS WOULD TRY TO UN-DERSTAND THE SALES PEOPLE MORE.
SALES ARE EARNED WITH LEGWORK. SHARING OPINIONS IS A WASTE OF TIME.
THE SALES PEOPLE LOOK DOWN ON THE ENGINEERS. IT'S AWFUL.
REVISITING THE MID-TERM BUSINESS PLAN? WHO HAS TIME FOR THAT?

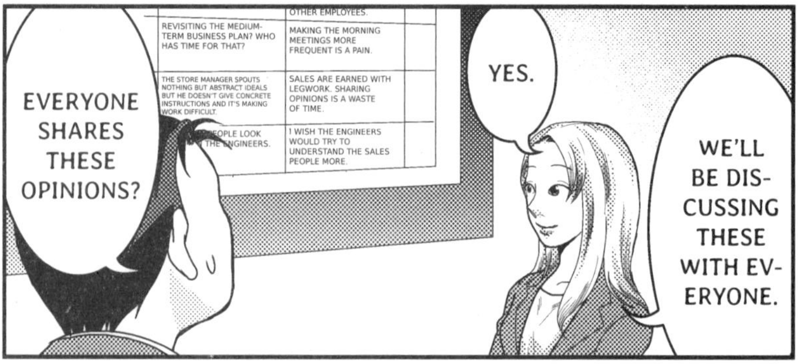
REVISITING THE MEDIUM-TERM BUSINESS PLAN? WHO HAS TIME FOR THAT?
MAKING THE MORNING MEETINGS MORE FREQUENT IS A PAIN.
THE STORE MANAGER SPOUTS NOTHING BUT ABSTRACT IDEALS BUT HE DOESN'T GIVE CONCRETE INSTRUCTIONS AND IT'S MAKING WORK DIFFICULT.
SALES ARE EARNED WITH LEGWORK. SHARING OPINIONS IS A WASTE OF TIME.
I WISH THE ENGINEERS WOULD TRY TO UNDERSTAND THE SALES PEOPLE MORE.
EVERYONE SHARES THESE OPINIONS?
YES.
WE'LL BE DIS-CUSSING THESE WITH EV-ERYONE.

CAN WE EVEN HOLD A DISCUSSION LIKE THIS?!

IT WILL TURN INTO A FIGHT, AND THINGS WILL ONLY GET WORSE!

PLEASE DON'T WORRY!

?!

I HAVE MY H
THINKING A
CLIENTS'
HAVE TIM
ABOUT M
WITH OTH

MAKING T
MEETINGS
FREQUENT

SALES ARE EA
LEGWORK. SHAR
IS A WASTE OF TIM

I WISH THE
ENGINEERS
WOULD TRY TO
UNDERSTAND THE
SALES PEOPLE
MORE.

I UNDER-STAND THIS CAN BE DIF-FICULT FOR YOU, SAKIGA-KE-SAN.

HOWEVER, FACING THIS KIND OF DIFFI-CULT SITUA-TION...

...THAT EVERYONE WOULD RATHER AVOID...

...AND DIS-CUSSING IT WITH EVERYONE IS CRITICAL.

THAT IS WHAT A SERIOUS DISCUSSION MEANS!

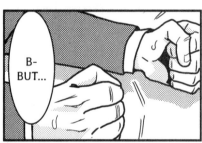

B-BUT...

IT'S ALL RIGHT. AT THIS STAGE, THERE'S NO NEED TO FORCE PEOPLE TO AGREE ON ONE OPINION ...

... AND THERE'S NO NEED TO DECIDE ANYTHING YET.

...AS I AM NOW, I DON'T HAVE THE CONFIDENCE TO CHANGE THEIR MINDS THROUGH DIS-CUSSION.

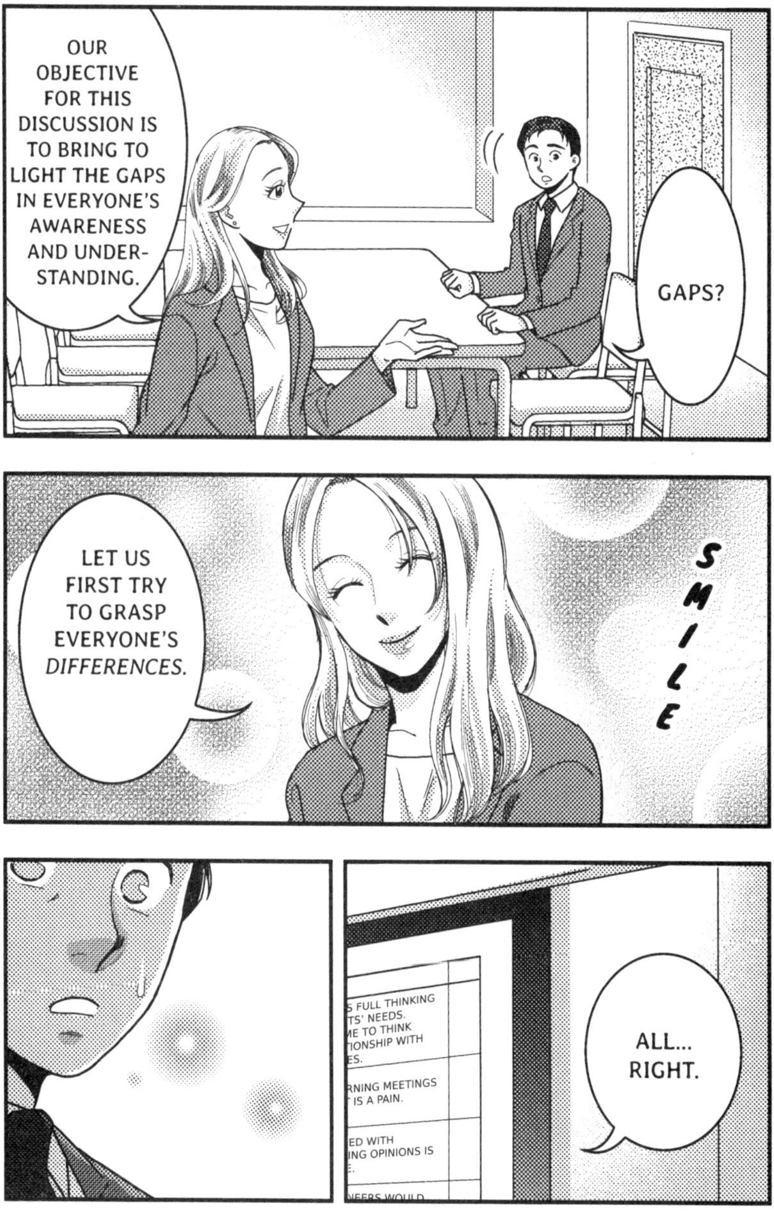
OUR OBJECTIVE FOR THIS DISCUSSION IS TO BRING TO LIGHT THE GAPS IN EVERYONE'S AWARENESS AND UNDER-STANDING.
GAPS?
LET US FIRST TRY TO GRASP EVERYONE'S *DIFFERENCES.*
SMILE
ALL... RIGHT.

THE NEXT DAY.

THANK YOU FOR SHARING YOUR VALUABLE OPINIONS WITH ME A FEW DAYS AGO.

REDUCE THE FREQUENCY OF MORNING MEETINGS.

SALES ARE EARNED WITH LEGWORK. SHARING OPINIONS IS A WASTE OF TIME.

I'D LIKE MORE CONCRETE INSTRUCTIONS OVER ABSTRACT IDEALS.

I'D RATHER THINK ABOUT TOMORROW'S NUMBERS, NOT 2-3 YEARS AHEAD.

I WANT TO RESOLVE OUR DISAGREEMENTS WITH THE ENGINEERS.

IT'S AWFUL THAT THE SALES PEOPLE LOOK DOWN ON THE ENGINEERS.

WE DON'T HAVE TIME TO REVISIT THE MEDIUM-TERM BUSINESS PLAN.

I HAVE MY HANDS FULL THINKING ABOUT MY CLIENTS' NEEDS.

TODAY, I'D LIKE TO SHARE WITH YOU THE OPINIONS THAT SEEM TO BE IMPORTANT FOR YOUR BRANCH.

WHISPER WAIT, PEOPLE REALLY SAID THAT?!

MUMBLE NO WAY!

MUMBLE

...

BASED ON THESE RESULTS, LET'S TRY SHARING HOW WE ALL FEEL REGARDING THE CURRENT SITUATION AT THIS STORE.

FIRST, LOOKING AT THESE RESULTS, CAN YOU SHARE HOW YOU USUALLY FEEL WORKING HERE DAILY?

SHARING THE DIFFERENCES IN HOW YOU FEEL IS ALSO IMPORTANT.

EVERYONE VIEWS THINGS DIFFERENTLY, AFTER ALL.

TO MAKE IT EASIER FOR EVERYONE TO TALK, I'VE PREPARED THESE GUIDELINES.

• DON'T REJECT ANYONE AND LISTEN TO EACH OTHER.
• DON'T TRY TO IDENTIFY WHO GAVE WHICH OPINION.
• SHARE YOUR HONEST EVERYDAY FEELINGS FOR THE SAKE OF A BETTER WORKPLACE FOR EVERYONE.

WELL, THEN. PLEASE SHARE YOUR FEELINGS ONE AT A TIME.

...

...

...

UM... DO I REALLY GO ON TOO MUCH ABOUT ABSTRACT IDEALS?

YOU, GO ANSWER HIM!

PUSH

UHH... WELL, YOU SEEM TO BE THE PASSIONATE TYPE...

...BUT IT'S HARD TO WORK WITH JUST MORNING MEETINGS AND ACTIVELY SHARING OPINIONS.

I THINK EVERYONE HAS THEIR HANDS FULL WITH THEIR OWN WORK. THIS GOES FOR ME AS WELL.

THERE'S SO MANY THINGS I WANT TO LEARN FROM EVERYONE... BUT IT'S HARD TO ASK.

IS THAT SO...

THANK YOU FOR SHARING YOUR FEELINGS TODAY, EVERYONE.

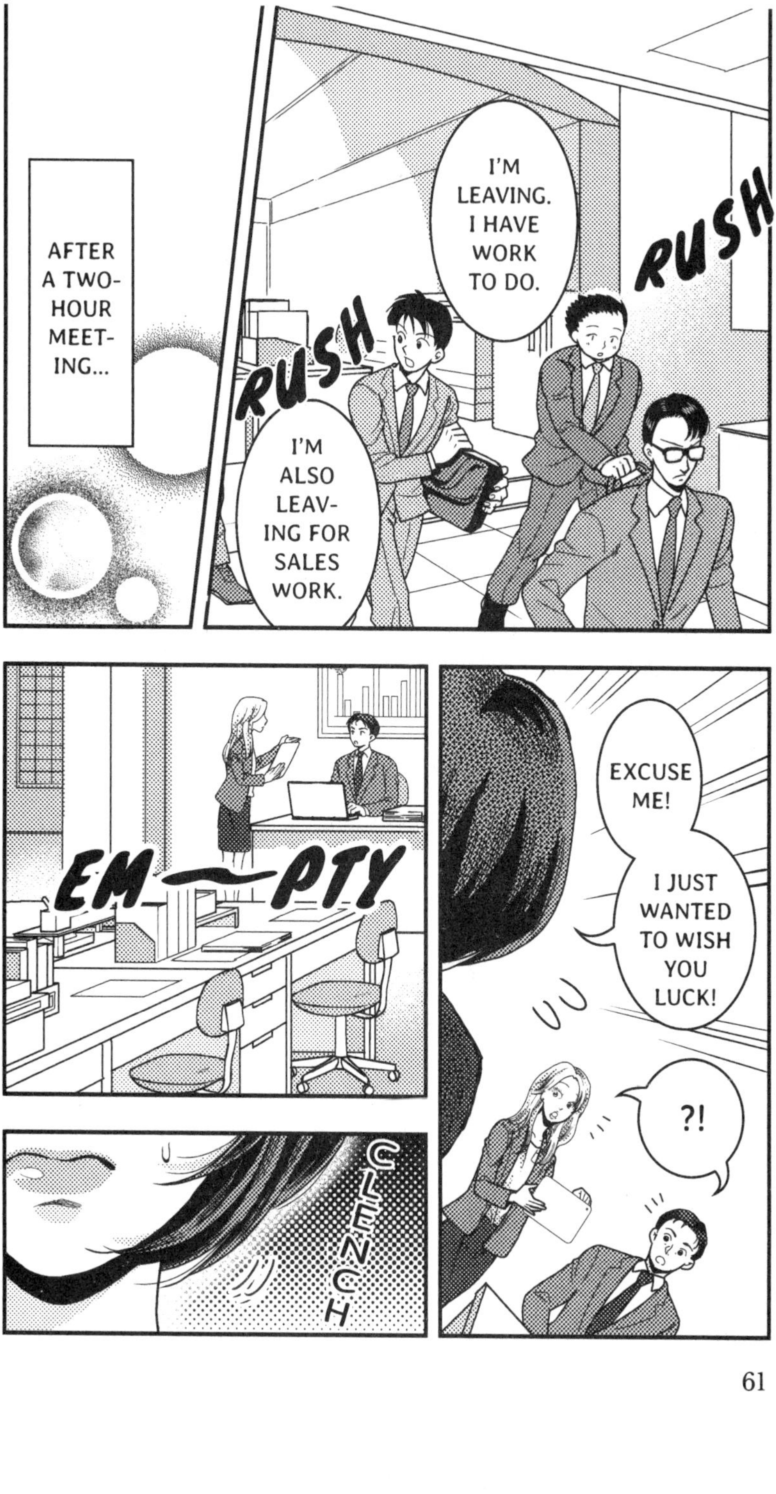

AFTER A TWO-HOUR MEETING...
I'M LEAVING. I HAVE WORK TO DO.
RUSH
RUSH
I'M ALSO LEAVING FOR SALES WORK.
EM—PTY
EXCUSE ME!
I JUST WANTED TO WISH YOU LUCK!
?!
CLENCH

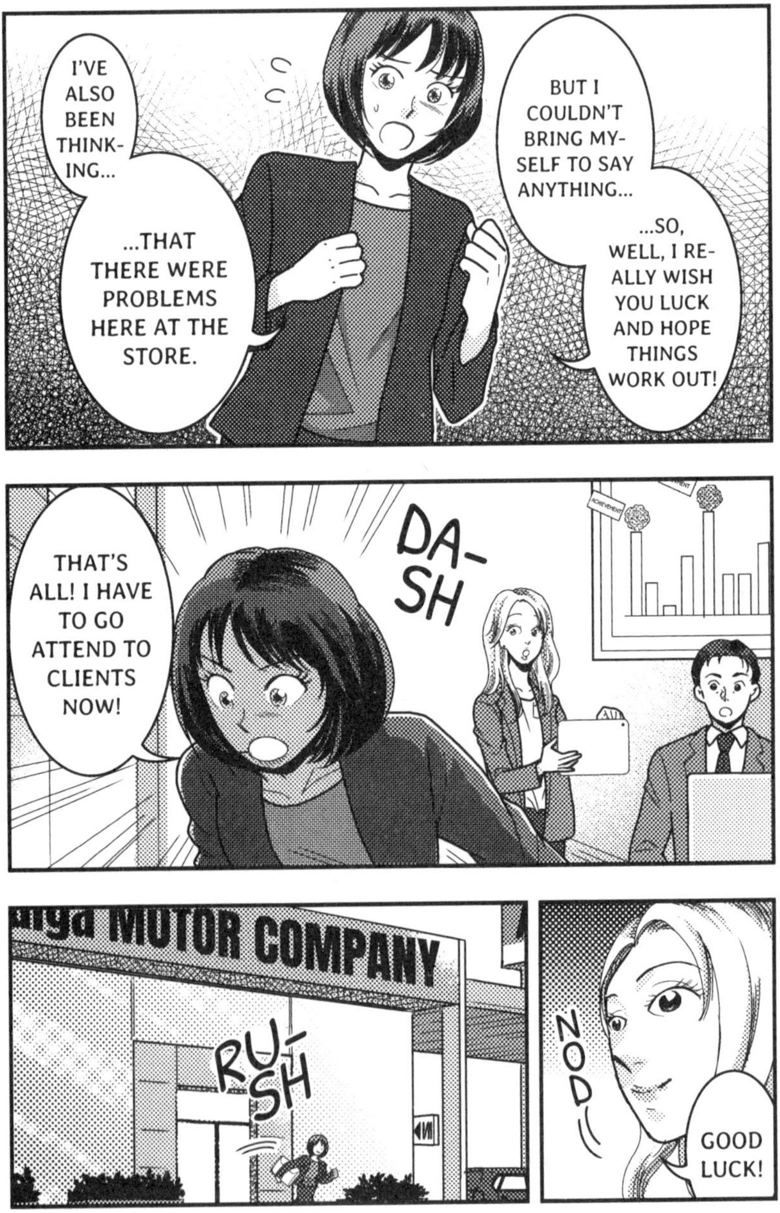
I'VE ALSO BEEN THINK-ING...
...THAT THERE WERE PROBLEMS HERE AT THE STORE.
BUT I COULDN'T BRING MY-SELF TO SAY ANYTHING...
...SO, WELL, I RE-ALLY WISH YOU LUCK AND HOPE THINGS WORK OUT!
THAT'S ALL! I HAVE TO GO ATTEND TO CLIENTS NOW!
DA-SH
MOTOR COMPANY
RU-SH
NOD
GOOD LUCK!

SAKIGA-KE-SAN!

LET'S BUILD A CORE TEAM!

A... CORE TEAM?

WE'LL THEN PROCEED WITH THIS CORE TEAM AT THE CEN-TER!

THIS STORE CAN CHANGE!

!

The store manager, Sakigake, consulted the Organization Development team from the head office's HR department and met one of their company's Organization Development facilitators, Mizushina. Sakigake learned from Mizushina what Organization Development is and how the process would go. He then agreed to first try the process with the sales department. In Organization Development, **obtaining the permission of a workplace, division, or organization's leader** is a very important step that must not be skipped.

Next, Mizushina, who is a third party in this situation, conducts a hearing where she asks employees at the store what they think about the branch. The results are anonymized and reported to the store manager. After this, the results are shown to all the sales department staff, and they hold a feedback meeting where they discuss these results. Ideally, in a feedback meeting, everyone will share their day-to-day feelings at work and engage in a **serious discussion**. The younger employees like Hanami and Hirose don't often get a chance to share their feelings. The feedback meeting gave them this chance and allowed them to give their opinions.

In the following pages, **we'll look at what Organization Development is, how the process goes, and what a serious discussion, a key component of Organization Development, is.**

...THAT EVERYONE WOULD RATHER AVOID...

...AND DISCUSSING IT WITH EVERYONE IS CRITICAL.

HOWEVER, FACING THIS KIND OF DIFFICULT SITUATION...

A discussion where everyone confronts the issues at hand is an essential step in the Organization Development process.

2-1 What Exactly Is Organization Development?

◆ Organization Development Is a "Label"

I also mentioned this in the Introduction of this book, but Organization Development doesn't refer to a single method. This makes it somewhat harder to grasp what Organization Development is exactly.

Similar to Human Resource Development, Career Development, and Psychotherapy, Organization Development is an accumulation of various theories and techniques that have all been wrapped up and bundled together under this one label (see Figure 2-1).

We often hear about Human Resource Development and Career Development in the workplace, so these terms see widespread usage and understanding. On the other hand, Organization Development is only starting to spread in mid-size and small companies, so a lot of people still have difficulty grasping what it actually is.

◆ Defining Organization Development

In the story, Mizushina from the head office Organization Development team explains to Sakigake that Organization Development is **an approach that takes into account the**

human side of organizations and workplaces. It takes into account the more obscure aspects on the human side of an organization or workplace, in order to see the situation better and make an effort to improve it.

Two central keywords in Organization Development are **discussion** and **cooperation.** Aiming toward a shared objective of improving the organization or workplace they're a part of, everyone engages in discussion focused on factors under the human side. From there, they formulate and execute a plan to help them cooperate better with one another.

The terms **"discussion"** and **"cooperation"** will keep coming up in this book. Another more concise way of defining Organization Development would be to call it a process of cultivating cooperation through discussion (building cooperative relationships).

A more academic definition is that Organization Development is an initiative that aims to improve a workplace or organization's **effectiveness, health, and ability to self-innovate.**

An organization is **effective** when its members are able to exhibit their full potential and are able to cooperate with each other. **Health** is determined by the members' satisfaction with the organization. In a healthy

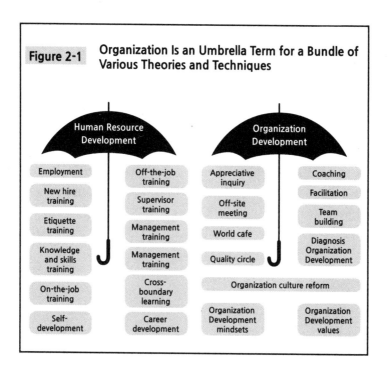

Figure 2-1	Organization Is an Umbrella Term for a Bundle of Various Theories and Techniques

Human Resource Development

Employment	Off-the-job training
New hire training	Supervisor training
Etiquette training	Management training
Knowledge and skills training	Management training
On-the-job training	Cross-boundary learning
Self-development	Career development

Organization Development

Appreciative inquiry	Coaching
Off-site meeting	Facilitation
World cafe	Team building
Quality circle	Diagnosis Organization Development

Organization culture reform

Organization Development mindsets	Organization Development values

organization, the members are highly motivated, healthy, and have good relationships with each other. The **ability to self-innovate** refers to the members' ability to assess their situation themselves and change for the better.

The word "development" in Organization Development invokes the idea of **progress, advancement, evolution, and growth,** and these are exactly the ideas that it aims for.

It might be easier to understand the concept by comparing it to human growth. A person is first born, goes through various experiences, and becomes an adult. If a person grows up well, they grow and develop into an effective and healthy human.

In this way, organizations are just like humans. By paying attention to the human side of organizations, good relationships are fostered between its members and it develops into an effective and healthy organization that's capable of self-innovation. That is what development is all about.

2-2 Steps in Organization Development

◆ How to Deal with Adaptive Challenges

As explained in the previous section, Organization Development is an approach that takes into account the human side of an organization or a workplace in order to improve it. Most of the issues that arise in the human side are ambiguous in nature, and the causes and solutions are not easily identifiable. As stated on page 43, the human side not only deals with technical problems, it usually involves adaptive challenges as well.

For these more obscure problems, it's hard to tell what exactly is going on within the organization or workplace (these are problems on the human side). Unlike with technical problems, directly applying existing solutions to these types of problems usually doesn't work. According to Heifetz, dealing with adaptive challenges requires the people involved to study and learn from the situation through discussion. By experiencing these types of situations, people's perceptions, assumptions, and habits can change.

Let's go back to the story for a bit and think about what happened. In the story, the store manager, Sakigake, tried to solve the lack of communication in their store by increasing the frequency of morning meetings and trying to hold a vision drafting workshop. However, these solutions didn't work. He treated the lack of communication as a superficial human-side problem and tried to directly apply standard solutions (morning meetings and vision drafting) to solve it. However, this communication problem is an obscure **adaptive challenge** that's happening on the human side between the store manager and staff. We can say that Sakigake tried to use solutions for a technical problem on an adaptive challenge and consequently failed. Aside from the lack of communication (and how this has become the norm), there are also other difficult problems, such as the high rate of days off and retirements. The store's fundamental problem hasn't actually been made clear yet. There is also a conflict between the employees, who believe that sharing opinions is unnecessary, and Sakigake, who wants everyone to interact more.

For an adaptive challenge like this where the problem is vague and the solution is unknown, Sakigake and the other employees will have to study what exactly is going on and find the fundamental problem. Through this, **they can deal with this adaptive challenge by changing the perception and belief (learning) that the lack of communication is normal and that sharing opinions is a waste of time.**

This is how the process of Organization Development goes. **The people involved deal with obscure human-side** problems by holding a discussion to study what is going on and try to find a way to solve the problem themselves.

A more concrete Organization Development process is introduced below.

◆ The Three Steps in Organization Development

The Organization Development process involves the team and people in the workplace talking with each other about obscure human-side problems. The three basic steps for this process are shown in Figure 2-2. These steps are **seeing the problem, serious discussion, and building a future.**

◆ Organization Development Step 1: Seeing the Problem

In the **seeing the problem** step, the people involved try to **make the obscure issues occurring on the human side of the organization visible.**

In the story, Mizushina of the Organization Development team holds a one-on-one hearing (**data gathering**) with the employees at the branch. The opinions and perceptions shared there were then anonymized and compiled (**data analysis**). The anonymized and compiled results were shown to the store manager and then presented to the employees (Mizushina's explanation at the beginning of their **feedback meeting**).

The issues on the human side are often hard to see, and people's perceptions and feelings regarding these issues usually vary from one person to another. By revealing these varying perceptions and viewpoints, the differences in people's feelings about and perceptions of the situation can be brought to light.

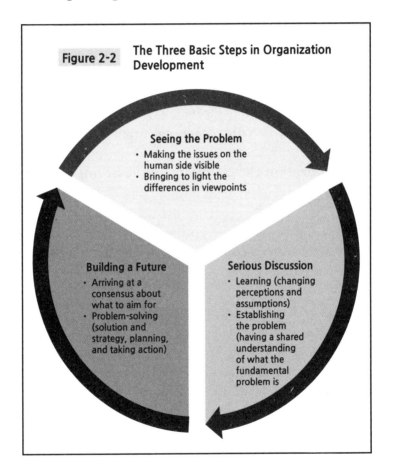

Figure 2-2 **The Three Basic Steps in Organization Development**

Seeing the Problem
- Making the issues on the human side visible
- Bringing to light the differences in viewpoints

Building a Future
- Arriving at a consensus about what to aim for
- Problem-solving (solution and strategy, planning, and taking action)

Serious Discussion
- Learning (changing perceptions and assumptions)
- Establishing the problem (having a shared understanding of what the fundamental problem is

In the story, in order to see the problem, Mizushina conducted one-on-one meetings with the employees to gather data. Often, results of other assessments (measuring employee satisfaction, stress check, survey of organizational climate) are also taken into account in the feedback meeting that's held after. Nowadays, it's also possible to conduct surveys via the Internet, and there are assessments that can be done separately by each workplace unit.

There is also a process that doesn't involve prior data gathering and analysis. These methods fall under **discussion-style Organization Development**. The people involved gather and discuss how they feel about the current situation at their workplace. At some point, they discuss in smaller groups and at others, they discuss with everyone involved.

◆ **Organization Development Step 2: Serious Discussion**

The next step is **serious discussion**. The objective of this step is **to learn what's necessary to deal with an adaptive challenge**. In other words, this

COULD YOU TELL ME WHAT YOU THINK ABOUT THIS BRANCH?

ANYTHING WILL DO, SO PLEASE DON'T HESITATE TO SHARE YOUR THOUGHTS.

The hearing that Mizushina conducts falls under data gathering.

step aims to **change people's perceptions and assumptions through discussion.**

For the store manager Sakigake, Hanami's comment in the feedback meeting about his instructions "making it hard to work" became an opportunity for him to realize how his way of doing things was perceived by his subordinates. This is an example of someone's perception of the situation changing through discussion.

In addition, during the serious discussion step, everyone tries to study the differences in viewpoints from the "seeing the problem" step. In this step, it's important to answer the question **"What is the fundamental problem?"** so that everyone can agree on what that is. That is to say, the aim is for everyone **to have a shared understanding on what the fundamental problem is in the situation they're facing.** Incidentally, they have yet to reach this point in Story 2.

Let's take the common situation below as an example and examine the reasons why establishing and having a shared understanding of the fundamental problem is necessary in order to move on to the next step.

Let's say that in a certain workplace, hardly anyone ever talks during meetings. They find out through a hearing that people think that it's hard to say anything with the atmosphere of the meetings, that the meetings tend to become one-on-one discussions between the manager and another member, that people tend to just listen to reports for the entire meeting, or that there's no point to gathering and talking as a group.

In the "seeing the problem" step, everyone's perception and viewpoint of the situation are made visible. There is of course sufficient significance in revealing the differences in everyone's perception of the more obscure human side of things. However, you cannot arrive at a solution just by seeing the problem. This is where the serious discussion step comes in. The objective of this step is ultimately for everyone to have a shared understanding of what kind of patterns and influences have led to the current situation. With this shared understanding, it is much easier to proceed to the next step (Building a Future).

In the earlier example, people thought that it was difficult to talk during meetings, so they just consisted of reports, which made them ineffective. The members should then investigate what is causing this through a serious discussion. They realize that the meetings have become a one-way

...BUT IT'S HARD TO WORK WITH JUST MORNING MEETINGS AND ACTIVELY SHARING OPINIONS.

Via their discussion, members are able to share opinions, learn, and realize things they normally wouldn't be able to in their everyday interactions.

communication filled with reports. People no longer have a shared objective in these meetings (filled with individual reports) and don't see the point to them, so they tend to just be passive participants. Supposing we realize all this, we will be able to identify that the fundamental problem with these meetings is that people don't think they are useful and therefore only participate passively in them, which they will have to change.

Once everyone has come to a common understanding of what the fundamental problem is (problem establishment), they can move on to the next step, building a future.

◆ Organization Development Step 3: Building a Future

Once everyone has a common understanding of the more obscure human-side challenge they're facing, they can proceed to the next step, **building a future** (the store employees haven't reached this stage in Story 2). In this step, everyone discusses how they intend to deal with the problem they identified in the serious discussion stage. They should then **come to a consensus on what kind of situation they'll be aiming for and how to bring it about.** For the first time, everyone will be thinking of a solution to the situation. They'll plan the approach they'll take as a group and actions each member will try **(planning**

the approach). After the approaches and actions have been decided, they will then proceed to implement them **(implementing the plan).**

In the example we looked at earlier, the members of the workplace have identified the problem: people don't understand the purpose of the meetings and consequently don't participate actively in them, which will need to change. In this stage, building a future, they will have to come to a consensus on what kind of result they'll be aiming for. They'll plan out what they need to do in order to bring that result about. Suppose they've agreed that they want to aim for energetic meetings where everyone can see their value, and actively work to make the situation better. They will then discuss and plan what they need to do (what actions and attitudes they have to take) in order to make their ideal meetings a reality. They can, for example, hold a discussion to make the objective of these meetings clearer. They can also resolve to express when this objective is not being met, while the meeting is ongoing. If they come to a consensus that these are the actions and attitudes they will be taking, they can implement their plans and, as a result, their meetings will begin to change.

Some time after these plans are implemented, they will go back to the first stage, seeing the problem, in order to assess the situation (how good the communication has become and to what extent people share the meeting's objective). This is called **evaluating the approach**. After this, they will then once again cycle through steps 1–3.

In the earlier example, one of the first problems expressed was that the atmosphere of the meetings made it hard to talk. If the people involved decided to think of a solution immediately after identifying this problem, they would've tried to think of how to improve the atmosphere of these meetings. They might decide to hold a drinking party in order to improve the meeting atmosphere. However, it's highly likely that nothing would changed in these meetings even if they implement this type of solution.

The process of studying the situation and identifying the fundamental problem together in the "serious discussion" step leads to being able to plan a meaningful solution in the "building a future" step.

The problems that we are trying to solve with Organization Development are obscure issues on the human side of the workplace. There are complex things going on within each and everyone's mind, and if you take the visible problem (like how there's little communication) to be the primary issue and try to solve that (say, through morning meetings), chances are things won't go very well. These kinds of problems require the people involved to study and learn together by discussing things with one another.

The following are issues that need to be tackled in these discussions.

① First, the people involved should try to see the problems that are more obscure and difficult to see.
② Next, they should have a serious discussion to change their assumptions and how they perceive the situation. From there they can then come to a consensus with everyone on what the fundamental problem is.
③ They should then come up with a plan together on how to deal with the identified problem (building a future).

People tend to immediately try and solve a problem when they see one. However, Organization Development poses that it's more difficult to properly identify and define the fundamental problem than to solve it. It emphasizes the importance of identifying what the fundamental problem is before trying to come up with a solution. Just as the above examples have shown us, when dealing with issues involving the human side of workplaces or organizations, **it is crucial to first confirm what the fundamental problem is (identifying and defining the problem) before trying to think of a solution (solving the problem).**

2-3　What Exactly Is a Discussion?

◆ Discussion Means Two-way Communication Where Meaning Is Conveyed

In sections 2-1 and 2-2, we kept using the term discussion. This discussion is one form of communication.

The word communication comes from Latin, and its original meaning was to share. That is to say, communication doesn't refer to the act of talking and listening. The true meaning of communication is to **share something among a group of people**.

One-way communication is one form of communication where a person A one-sidedly tells person B something. The other is a two-way communication where persons A and B talk back and forth with each other. One-way communication includes information dissemination, reports, and lectures while a common form of two-way communication is a discussion.

A discussion is a **two-way communication where meaning is conveyed**. The meaning behind the words exchanged between multiple people and how their significance changes is important in a discussion.

People instantly attach meanings to various things the moment they encounter them. For example, when people hear that a colleague of theirs has resigned and they don't know the reason (based on what they know), some will think that their colleague left for a better job somewhere else, while others will think that they must have been having a hard time with work at their company. Just like this, we constantly attach our own meaning and significance to things and happenings around us. The way people come up with these meanings also varies from person to person. This means that **we don't live in an objective world but in a subjective one that's based on our own chosen meanings.**

This idea of attaching our own meanings to things doesn't usually come up in daily conversation, so people don't normally realize that this is the case. In contrast, **during discussions, people talk about the meaning and intent within their words so this meaning is shared and conveyed.** Applying this to the resignation example, a discussion won't stop at the word "resignation" (the reality). The discussion will also clarify that the person resigned because they were having a hard time because the work environment was very tense. A discussion begins by including the meaning and circumstances (intent) behind that colleague's resignation. Thus, the person who thought that their colleague resigned to transfer to a better job may realize that they made a wrong assumption and change the meaning they attached to this event. They might then realize that their colleague resigned due to the tense atmosphere at their workplace. There is also a possibility that this meaning will evolve to include the idea that if the tense atmosphere at work doesn't change, even more people might resign or go on leave. Once people think that their colleague's resignation concerns them, chances are high that their perception of the current situation will change. The meaning and intent behind words were shared and conveyed and, as a result, the meaning the person attached to these words in the example changed. **This kind of two-way communication, where the meaning that people attach to words can change, is called a discussion.**

◆ The Four Levels of Two-way Communication

There are **four levels** to two-way communication (see Figure 2-4). In order to better understand what a discussion is, we'll be taking a look at each individually.

In this model, the two types of discussions are the **introspective discussion** and the **productive discussion**. According to this model, a first-time discussion starts with the ① **polite conversation level**. It then moves on to the following stages, in order from ② **debate**, ③ **introspective discussion**, and finally to ④ **productive discussion**.

Figure 2-3   A Discussion is a Two-way Communication Where Meaning Is Conveyed

Information Dissemination, Reports, Lectures, etc.: One-way Communication

Discussion: A Two-way Communication Where Meaning Is Conveyed

Words + Meaning   Word + Meaning

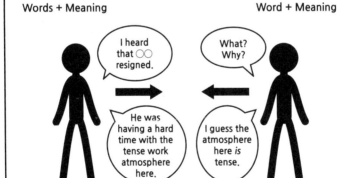

Figure 2-4　The Four Stages of Two-way Communication

Level 4: Productive Discussion

Exchange　　　　: Inquiry toward the future, slowly.

Speaking style　: New insights and ideas are discussed (produced).

Listening style　: Listening to the whole, no boundaries.

Meaning　　　　: Changes, new meanings are produced.

Level 1: Polite Conversation

Exchange　　　　: Polite and careful.

Speaking style　: One particular person talks.
　　　　　　　　　Honest opinions are not shared.

Listening style　: Downloading (taking in what others say).
　　　　　　　　　There are times when no one reacts.

Meaning　　　　: Focused on the initial meaning attached.

Level 3: Introspective Discussion

Exchange	:	Inquiry into concerned parties.
Speaking style	:	Introspective.
Listening style	:	Empathizing with what the other party says. Listening to one's inner voice.
Meaning	:	Changes through discussion.

Exchange	:	Debate, conflict.
Speaking style	:	Frank. Being assertive with your feelings / beliefs.
Listening style	:	Listening to outside sources. Listening to make a judgment.
Meaning	:	Focused on the initial meaning attached.

◆ Level 1: Polite Conversation

Most conversations between people who hardly know each other are polite but superficial and sometimes insincere. People do not feel safe and secure enough to share their honest opinions, so they only talk about superficial things. One person tends to talk the most, and everyone avoids saying anything risky.

The listening style for this level is called "downloading," as coined by Otto Scharmer. Think of this behavior as similar to when a smartphone automatically downloads an app. The words of the person speaking are filtered through the listener's experiences and assumptions.

A boss giving her subordinates directions usually falls in this class of polite conversations. In the story, when Sakigake started holding the morning meetings, he asked Akemoto whether this was all right. Akemoto didn't give his honest opinion and instead agreed only superficially. This is an example of a polite conversation.

In polite conversations, people only hear what they want to hear, the way they want to hear it. As such, the meaning behind the words is not shared. A discussion where the meaning attached by the listener changes does not occur at this stage. Let's consider a situation in a manufacturing factory where a previous document was changed for safety purposes. The boss will say that "the form has been changed, so from today we'll be using the new one." The subordinate will have no choice but to agree.

In a polite conversation like this, the instances surrounding the situation (why the form was changed, what problems had occurred with the previous form, etc.) are not shared with the subordinate. The subordinate then proceeds into downloading mode and attaches their own meaning to the change (for example, there are probably people who will think that this change was unnecessary). In this situation, the subordinate won't be satisfied with the meaning behind the change and will feel like they were forced to use this new form (the chances that they will use the new form effectively is low).

Even worse than this situation is when the subordinate actually asks the reason for the change and the boss only answers that it was a decision by the higher-ups. This indicates that even the boss doesn't know the meaning behind the change. In this kind of workplace, the subordinate will feel that there is no use saying anything to their boss and they will never get past the polite conversation level. Polite conversation cannot lead to changes.

I DON'T MIND ANYTHING AS LONG AS THE NUMBERS GO UP.

WHAT DO YOU THINK, AKEMO-TO-SAN?

It would be difficult to change if everyone stays at the polite conversation level.

It would be difficult to change if everyone stays at the polite conversation level, and as a result, the dissatisfaction over the meaning behind using the new form (the intent, objective, and problems addressed by changing the form) remains. and this situation doesn't change.

◆ Level 2: Debate

Once the parties involved are able to share their honest opinions, they will tend to insist on their point of view when faced with a different one. This level of discussion is the debate level. Let us go back to the example about the safety form change. Let's say that when they were deciding whether or not to change the form, person A wanted to change it while person B wanted to continue using the current one. This kind of communication where people have to decide on one opinion or the other is called a debate. The exchange becomes focused on who is right (who wins) and the surrounding people listen to the conversation as outsiders to judge who is right or wrong. This type of communication is often seen in business settings.

A discussion isn't merely a flow of details from words, it's a form of communication where meaning is shared and possibly changed. However, in a debate, the people involved insist on their own assumptions and opinions, so there is no way that this can lead to a change in their assumptions or in the meaning that they've initially attached to the situation.

In contrast, beyond the topic of whether or not the form should be changed, if the people involved instead talk about the problems that were found in the current form and the objectives for changing it, their conversation will move up to the discussion level. At this level, the meaning behind the form change can be shared between them. This way, people with differing opinions can come to an agreement since they now share the same knowledge of the circumstances behind the change and can judge from the same point of view.

◆ Level 3: Introspective Discussion

In the debate level, the parties involved will insist on their own viewpoint, but once they are able to see things from the viewpoint of the other party, they will then have moved up to the introspective discussion level. This is an exchange where the parties involved try to inquire about what the other is thinking or about the other party themselves and sympathetically listen to what they have to say. At the same time, at this level, the people involved also reflect on their own thoughts and views. For example, when thinking about whether or not the safety form should be changed, a person can think about what assumptions and intentions they are basing their opinion on. They will think about what changing or not changing the sheet will mean to them and converse with the other party while reflecting on these matters.

In the introspective discussion stage, the parties involved do not insist that their own opinion is right. They take it to be their hypothesis at the moment and understand that it can still change.

In Story 2, Hanami shares that it can be hard to work with the morning meetings and the store manager's insistence on actively sharing opinions. When Sakigake hears this, he doesn't stick to his opinion that holding morning meetings is essential (that he's doing the right thing as the store manager). Because of this, he was able to listen to Hanami's thoughts and sympathize with him. (If Sakigake didn't only respond with an agreement here and instead also shared his own thoughts, this introspective discussion could've been taken one step further.) As the story shows, sympathizing with opinions and thoughts that are different from yours is a very important attitude in both discussions and Organization Development as a whole.

◆ **Level 4: Productive Discussion**

In the introspective discussion stage, a person is able to look at the differences between themselves and others and is able to hold a sympathetic and understanding exchange with them. One level above this is the productive discussion level. At this level, one is able to look toward the future that is best for the whole group or organization and cross the boundaries between oneself and others (depending on the situation, this can be between one's department and another). In this kind of exchange, new findings, ideas, mindsets, and meanings

IS THAT SO...

Listening sympathetically made it possible for Sakigake to reflect upon himself.

are discovered. In the case of the safety form, the discussion will focus on aiming for a better and safer workplace for everyone. The discussion moves beyond just the question of whether or not the safety form should be changed. Instead, it focuses on discussing how to more effectively manage safety in the workplace and studies what needs to be done to achieve this. This kind of discussion where new ideas are born from conversation is a productive discussion.

◆ Discussion Levels and the Three Steps of Organization Development

We discussed earlier that there are three steps in Organization Development: seeing the problem, serious discussion, and building a future. In the serious discussion step, people will need to engage in introspective discussion, and in the building a future step, they will need to engage in productive discussion. First, in the serious discussion process, you establish the fundamental problem in the situation that you and other people are facing within a workplace or organization. From here, there is a need to change your views and the meanings you attach to the current situation. To do this, you will first need to set aside your own view (hypothesis) and listen carefully and reflect on what other people have to say in order to understand how you're influencing the people around you. This kind of introspective discussion is crucial for this step.

Next, in the building a future step, you will have to make plans on what attitude and action to take in order to achieve the best future for your workplace or organization as a whole. By engaging in a productive discussion at this step, you will discover new views and ideas that you weren't able to see before.

To be able to engage in productive discussion, you will have to overcome the boundaries between yourself and other people (or your department and other departments, depending on the situation) and be able to share a view of the future that's best for the workplace or organization as whole. You'll discuss what approaches and actions you need to take in order to achieve the future that the entire group wants to reach. This discussion will give birth to new views, ideas, and approaches that you will then have to implement. Depending on the situation, you may even take on the challenge of tackling some harder-to-solve issues in the workplace.

Part 2

The Core Team as an Agent of Change

STORY 3
BUILDING A CORE TEAM

A CORE TEAM?

YES!

IN THE HEARING A FEW DAYS AGO, THE PROBLEMS THIS STORE IS FACING BECAME A BIT CLEARER.

THE CORE TEAM WILL BE DEALING WITH THOSE.

AREN'T THE TWO OF US ENOUGH TO DEAL WITH THIS?

NO.

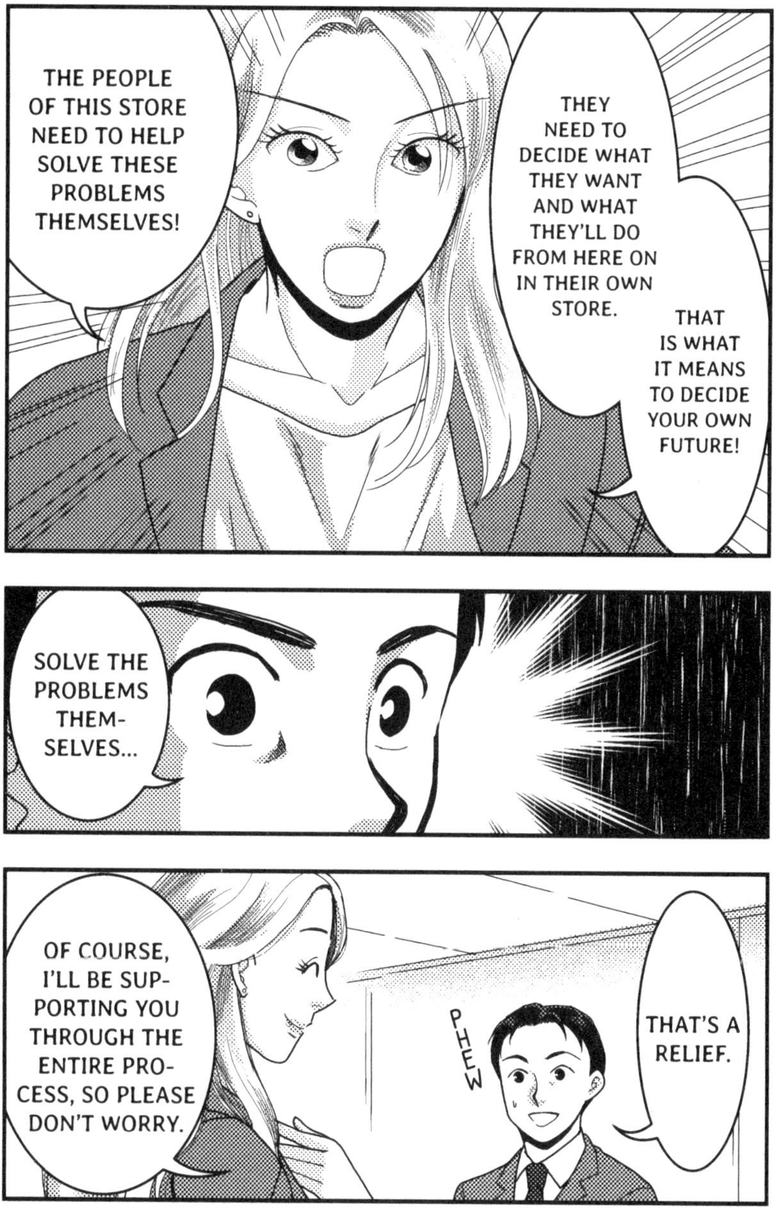
THE PEOPLE OF THIS STORE NEED TO HELP SOLVE THESE PROBLEMS THEMSELVES!
THEY NEED TO DECIDE WHAT THEY WANT AND WHAT THEY'LL DO FROM HERE ON IN THEIR OWN STORE.
THAT IS WHAT IT MEANS TO DECIDE YOUR OWN FUTURE!
SOLVE THE PROBLEMS THEM-SELVES...
OF COURSE, I'LL BE SUP-PORTING YOU THROUGH THE ENTIRE PRO-CESS, SO PLEASE DON'T WORRY.
PHEW
THAT'S A RELIEF.

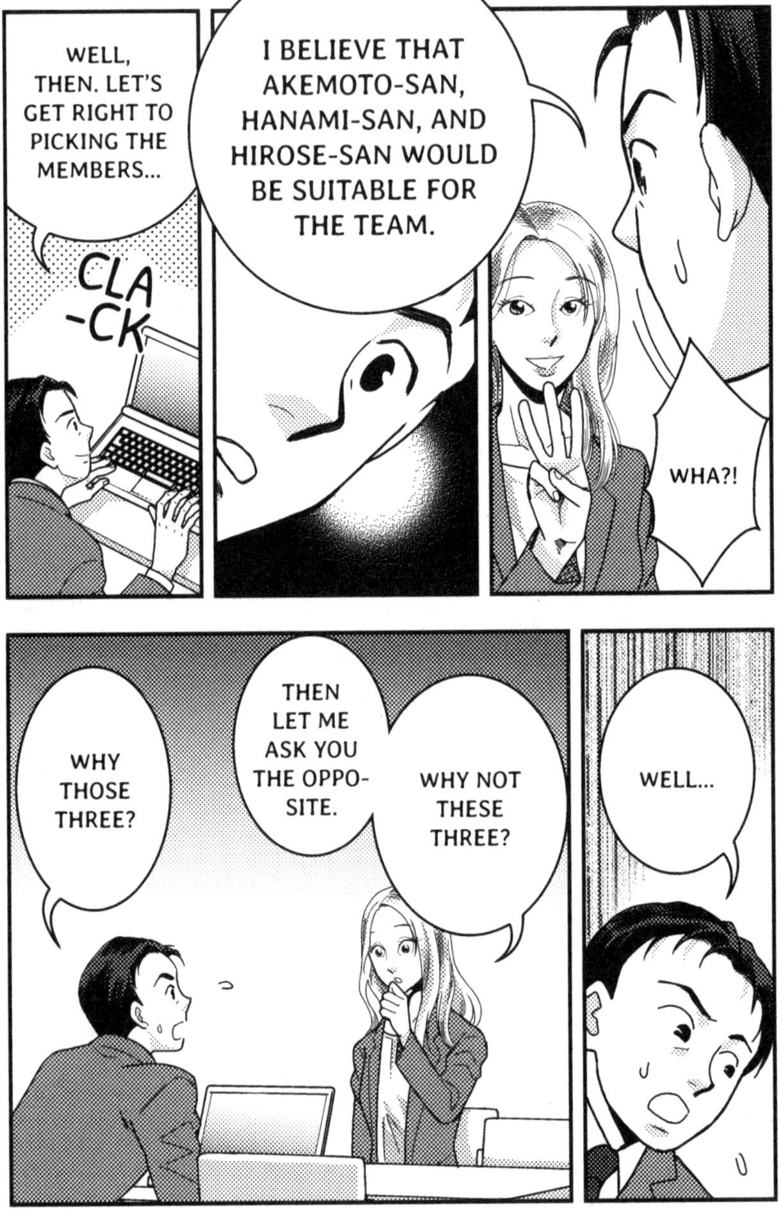
WELL, THEN. LET'S GET RIGHT TO PICKING THE MEMBERS...
CLA -CK
I BELIEVE THAT AKEMOTO-SAN, HANAMI-SAN, AND HIROSE-SAN WOULD BE SUITABLE FOR THE TEAM.
WHA?!
WHY THOSE THREE?
THEN LET ME ASK YOU THE OPPO- SITE.
WHY NOT THESE THREE?
WELL...

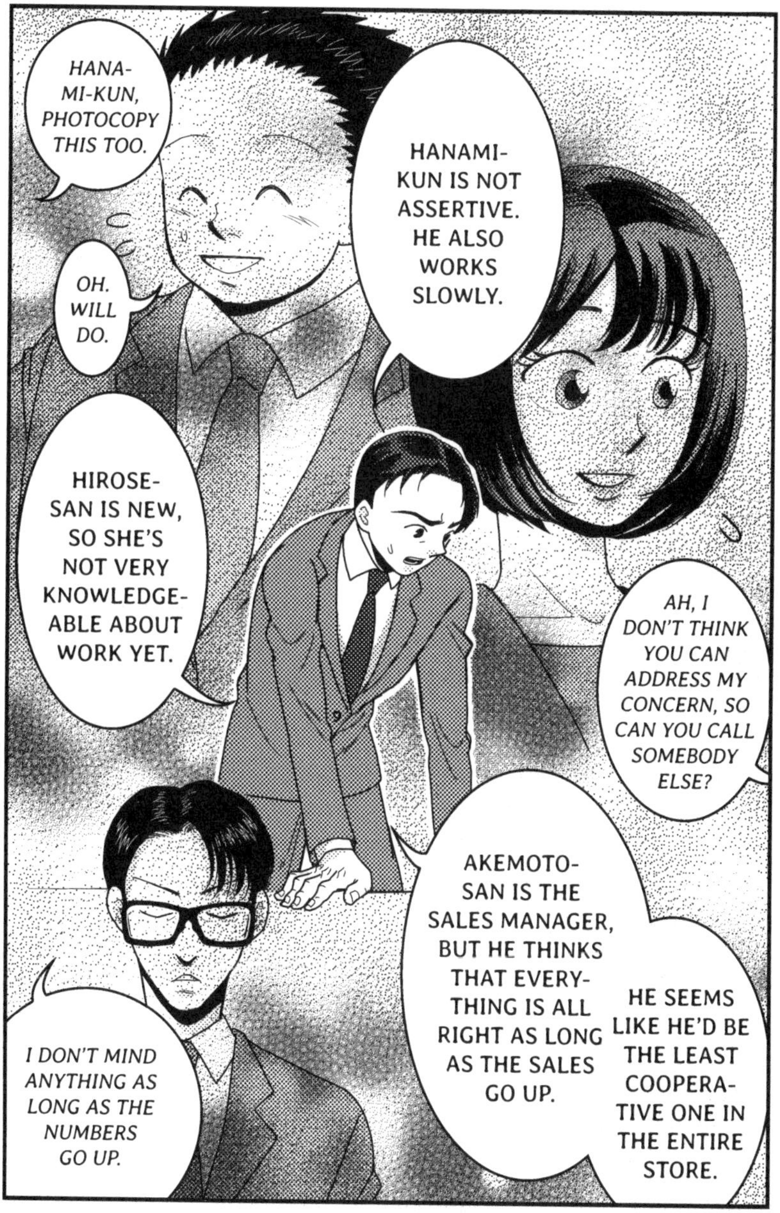
HANA-MI-KUN, PHOTOCOPY THIS TOO.
HANAMI-KUN IS NOT ASSERTIVE. HE ALSO WORKS SLOWLY.
OH. WILL DO.
HIROSE-SAN IS NEW, SO SHE'S NOT VERY KNOWLEDGE-ABLE ABOUT WORK YET.
AH, I DON'T THINK YOU CAN ADDRESS MY CONCERN, SO CAN YOU CALL SOMEBODY ELSE?
AKEMOTO-SAN IS THE SALES MANAGER, BUT HE THINKS THAT EVERY-THING IS ALL RIGHT AS LONG AS THE SALES GO UP.
HE SEEMS LIKE HE'D BE THE LEAST COOPERA-TIVE ONE IN THE ENTIRE STORE.
I DON'T MIND ANYTHING AS LONG AS THE NUMBERS GO UP.

I SEE.

IF THAT'S THE CASE...

...THEN I BELIEVE YOU FIRST NEED TO LEARN TO UNDERSTAND THE HEARTS OF THE PEOPLE IN FRONT OF YOU, SAKIGAKE-SAN.

I...DO?

YES. PLEASE RECALL HIROSE-SAN FROM JUST A WHILE AGO.

...YOU HAVE MY FULL SUPPORT!

EVEN THOUGH THINGS AREN'T GOING VERY WELL, SHE STILL WENT OUT OF HER WAY TO SHOW HER SUPPORT FOR US.

SEEING HER TALK THAT WAY, I WAS SURE OF IT.

THIS STORE CAN CHANGE!

!

DOES THIS MEAN I HAVEN'T UNDERSTOOD ANY OF THEM ALL ALONG?

SMILE

NOW THAT YOU'VE CONSIDERED THAT...

...MAYBE YOU CAN TRY LOOKING AT THEM FROM A DIFFERENT POINT OF VIEW FROM NOW ON.

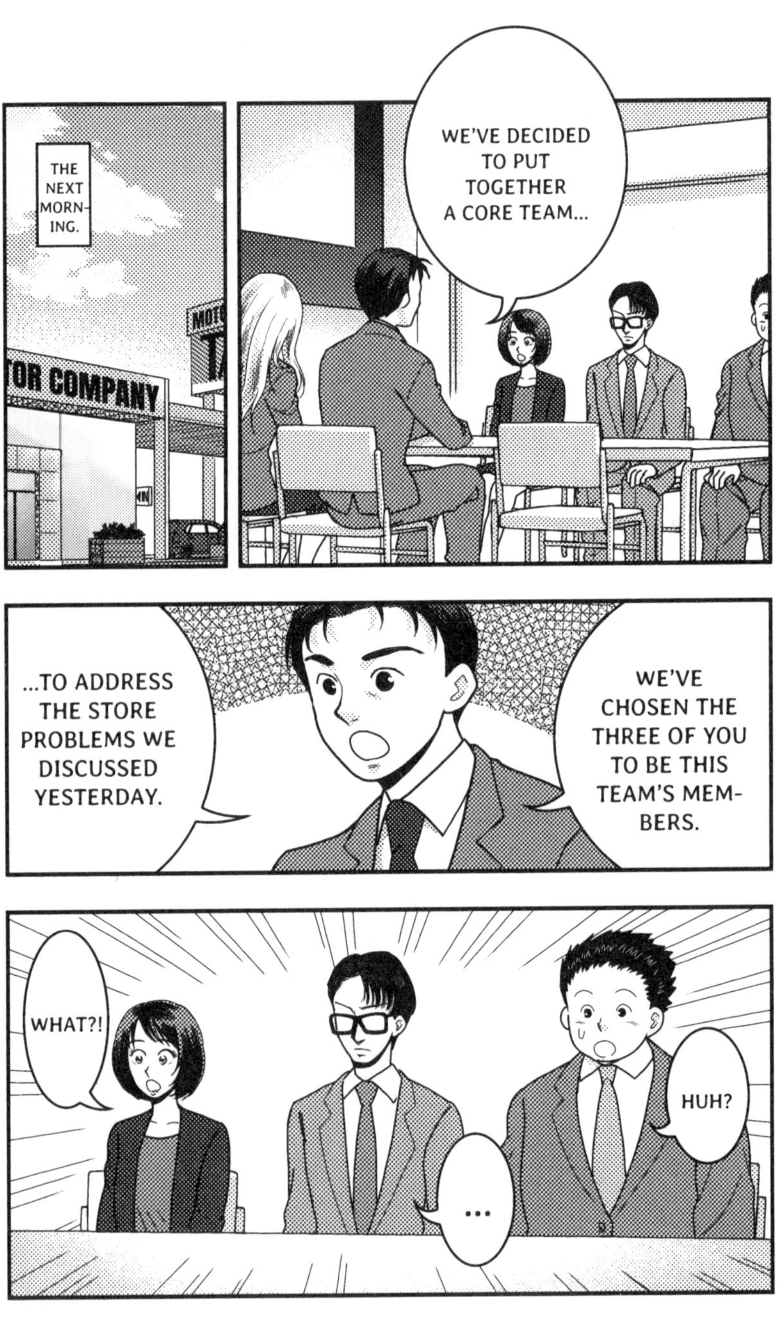

THE NEXT MORNING.
COMPANY
WE'VE DECIDED TO PUT TOGETHER A CORE TEAM...
...TO ADDRESS THE STORE PROBLEMS WE DISCUSSED YESTERDAY.
WE'VE CHOSEN THE THREE OF YOU TO BE THIS TEAM'S MEMBERS.
WHAT?!
...
HUH?

UMM.... SO, WHAT SHOULD WE DO?

THAT'S SOMETHING YOU'LL HAVE TO DECIDE FOR YOURSELF. IT WON'T BE DICTATED BY YOUR MANAGER.

OH...

DO YOU HAVE ANY OTHER QUESTIONS? COMMENTS?

HOW ABOUT YOU, AKEMOTO-SAN...?

I'LL COMPLY WITH WHATEVER YOU DECIDE.

101

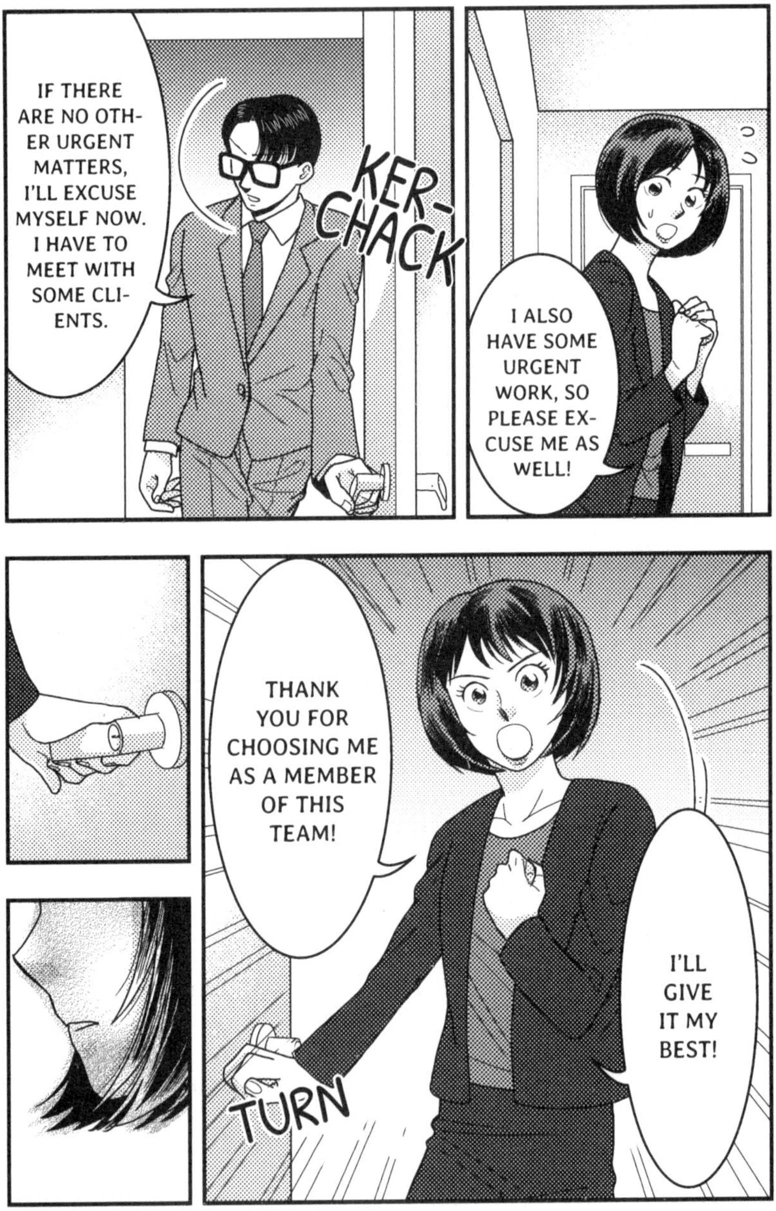
IF THERE ARE NO OTHER URGENT MATTERS, I'LL EXCUSE MYSELF NOW. I HAVE TO MEET WITH SOME CLIENTS.
KER-CHACK
I ALSO HAVE SOME URGENT WORK, SO PLEASE EXCUSE ME AS WELL!
THANK YOU FOR CHOOSING ME AS A MEMBER OF THIS TEAM!
I'LL GIVE IT MY BEST!
TURN

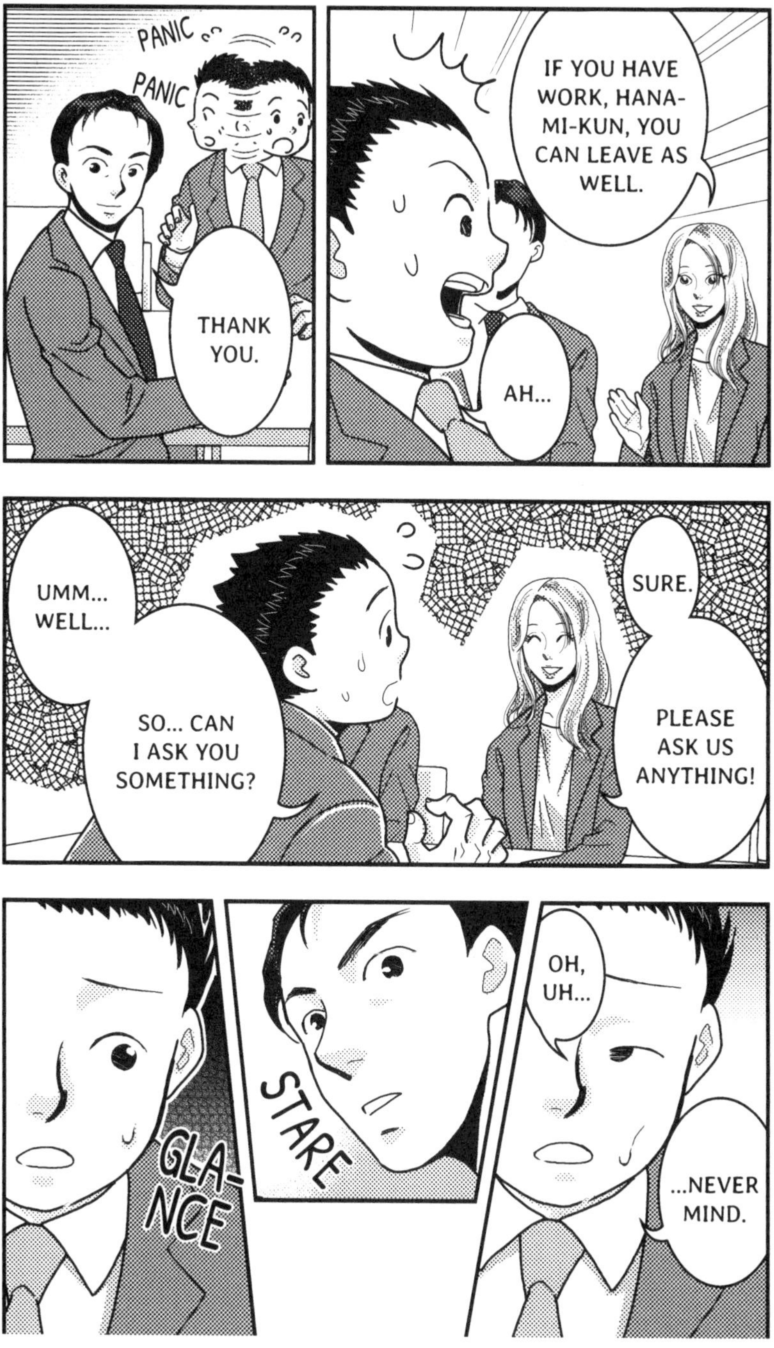
PANIC
PANIC
THANK YOU.
IF YOU HAVE WORK, HANA-MI-KUN, YOU CAN LEAVE AS WELL.
AH...
UMM... WELL...
SO... CAN I ASK YOU SOMETHING?
SURE.
PLEASE ASK US ANYTHING!
GLA-NCE
STARE
OH, UH...
...NEVER MIND.

IT'S ALL RIGHT, IT'S NOTHING...

...I'LL DO WHATEVER IS NEEDED...

BOW

I'LL BE HEADING BACK TO WORK NOW.

SLAM

...

SAKI-GAKE-SAN...

...IF YOU'RE WORRIED ABOUT HANA-MI-SAN, YOU SHOULD TRY APPROACHING HIM YOUR-SELF!

THIS IS A CHANCE FOR YOU TO TRY AND UNDER-STAND ANOTH-ER PERSON'S THOUGHTS.

AHH!

CAN I SIT WITH YOU?

S-SIR!

GHAK!

A-ARE YOU OKAY?!

HERE! DRINK THIS TEA!

THUMP THUMP

GULP
GULP
GULP
GULP

SORRY ABOUT THAT. THANK YOU!

PHEW

YOU SHOULD SLOW IT DOWN A BIT.

TH-THAT'S A LOT OF FOOD, THOUGH.

HE'S ALSO QUITE BULKY. I WONDER IF HE DOES SPORTS OR SOMETHING.

CAN YOU LET ME KNOW WHAT THAT WAS?

SO, ANY-WAY...

YES?

BITE

CHEW

...I BELIEVE YOU WANT-ED TO ASK A QUESTION EARLIER.

...

WHY...

...DID YOU PICK ME TO BE A MEMBER?

WELL...

... I'VE BEEN OBSERVING YOU, AND YOU SEEM TO GET ALONG WITH OTHERS AND WORK WELL IN A TEAM.

BUT... THAT'S ONLY BECAUSE EVERYONE SEES ME AS SOMEONE WHO'S EASY TO USE.

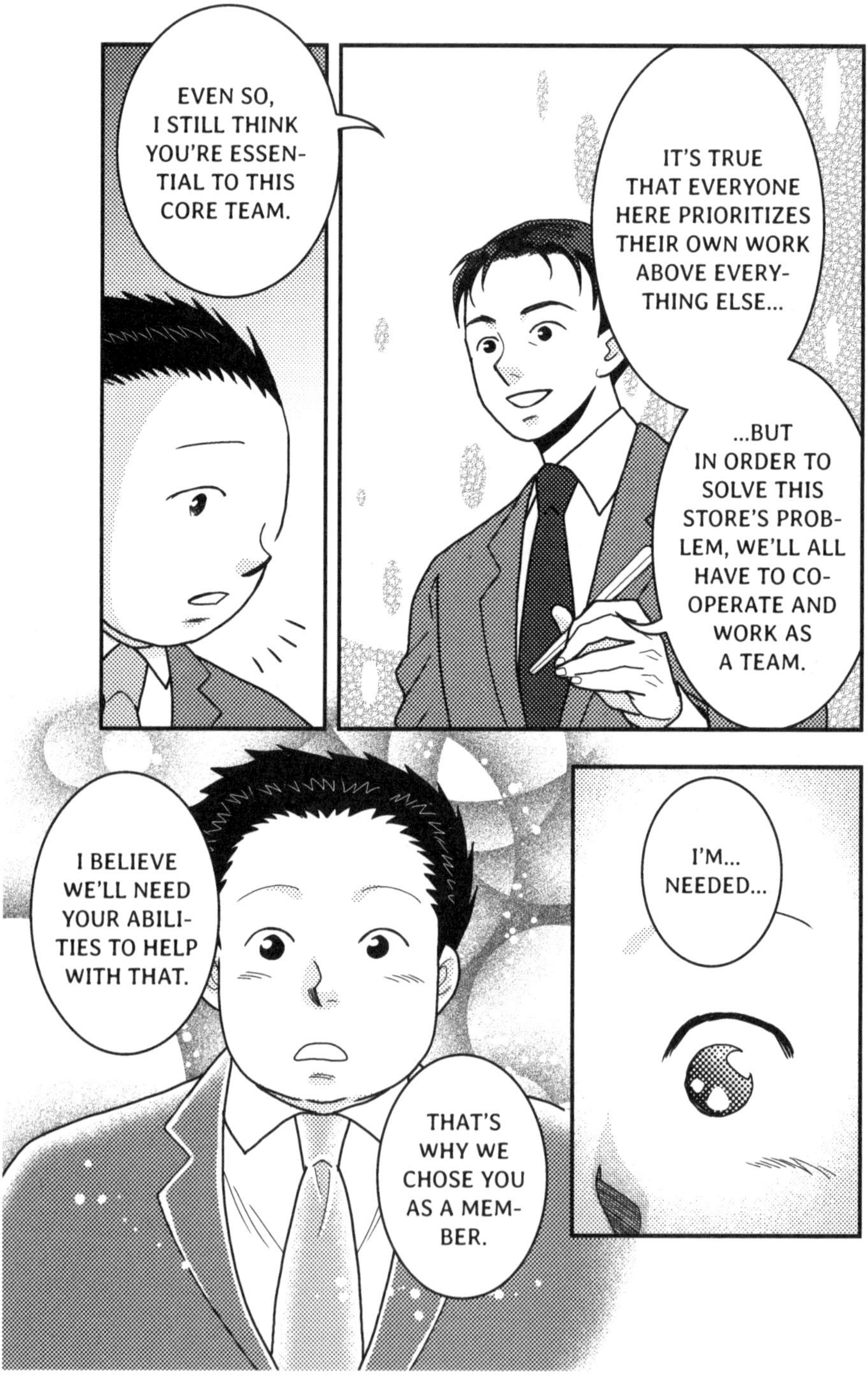
EVEN SO, I STILL THINK YOU'RE ESSENTIAL TO THIS CORE TEAM.
IT'S TRUE THAT EVERYONE HERE PRIORITIZES THEIR OWN WORK ABOVE EVERYTHING ELSE...
...BUT IN ORDER TO SOLVE THIS STORE'S PROBLEM, WE'LL ALL HAVE TO COOPERATE AND WORK AS A TEAM.
I BELIEVE WE'LL NEED YOUR ABILITIES TO HELP WITH THAT.
THAT'S WHY WE CHOSE YOU AS A MEMBER.
I'M... NEEDED...

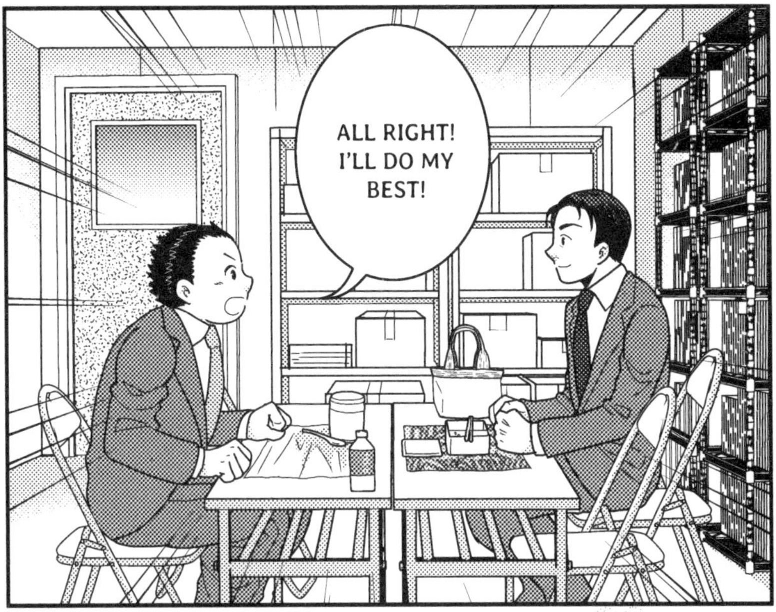
ALL RIGHT! I'LL DO MY BEST!

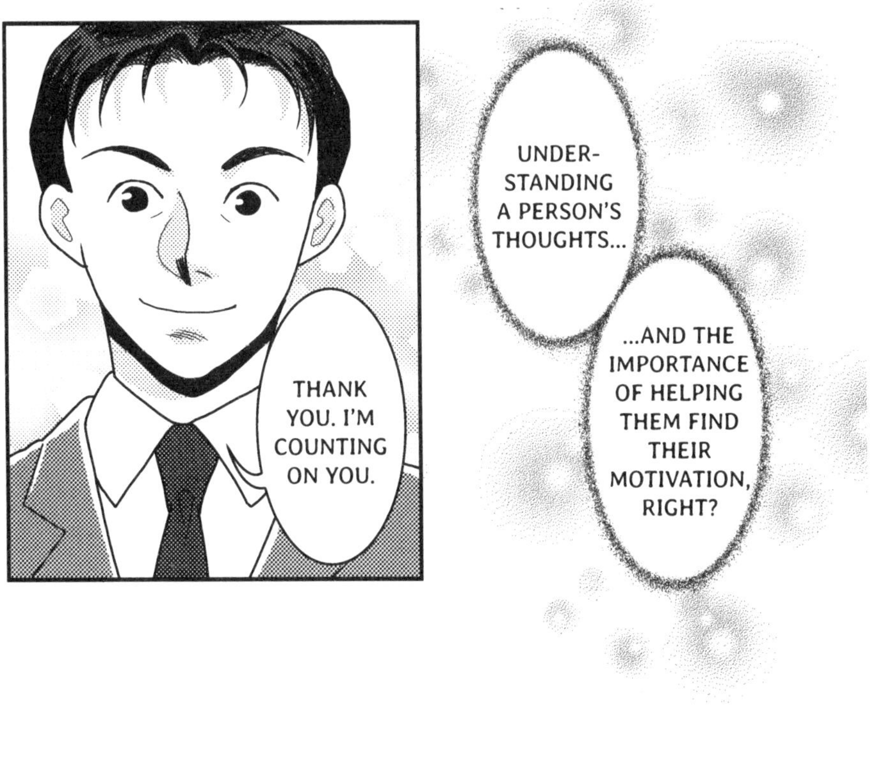
UNDER-STANDING A PERSON'S THOUGHTS...
...AND THE IMPORTANCE OF HELPING THEM FIND THEIR MOTIVATION, RIGHT?
THANK YOU. I'M COUNTING ON YOU.

In order to improve the branch, a core team was formed. It was decided that this core team will now lead the transformation project. Up until now (Story 2), the center of the project had been the store manager, Sakigake, and the Organization Development facilitator, Mizushina. In Story 3, the members of the core team—the newbie Hirose and the young employee, Hanami—were both highly motivated to participate in this transformation project. The circle of people who are driving the Organization Development is getting bigger.

At the same time, it's now becoming more difficult to identify who really is the main character of the story, isn't it?

For Organization Development to progress, **you'll need various people to play various roles.** There isn't one main character who ends up improving the workplace or organization. **In an Organization Development story, the number of main characters will keep increasing until everyone becomes a main character (all the people concerned).** This progress reflects the process of Organization Development better.

In this part, we will look at why it's important for everyone to become a concerned party when it comes to Organization Development. We'll also take a look at what kind of people are needed and what kind of roles they have to play in order to push Organization Development forward.

3-1 The Importance of Trying to See What You Can't See

◆ The Difficulty of Trying to Understand the Feelings of Someone Before You

The store manager, Sakigake, was told by the Organization Development team member, Mizushina, that he **needed to learn to understand the hearts of the people who are right in front of him.** When you read the lines in that scene, how does it personally make you feel?

If you thought the same was true for you or that you've also had similar experiences as Sakigake, that is a good sign. It's proof that you're trying to see what you can't yet see. On the other hand, if you thought that you're already able to understand people's feelings, then that may be a red flag. You might need to reconsider your evaluation.

...THEN I BELIEVE YOU FIRST NEED TO LEARN TO UNDERSTAND THE HEARTS OF THE PEOPLE WHO ARE RIGHT IN FRONT OF YOU, SAKIGAKE-SAN.

At the start of the story, we can say that Sakigake also wasn't able to see the human side of the workplace yet.

We've all faced problems and challenges in school or at work. Through those experiences, we learn

---

how important it is to look carefully so we understand what these problems are truly all about.

We are also unable to look at too many things at the same time. That means that as a result of learning to look carefully at our work or assignments, we then tend to lose sight of the feelings of the people around us.

For example, in meetings, people will often talk about the numbers that pertain to achievement targets and results. They will often discuss how to achieve these results or how to solve problems related to work. As seen in the iceberg analogy in Figure 1-2 on page 37, people will often discuss the things above the water (the hard side of the workplace), but will spend very little time discussing the human side (each person's awareness and motivation, the communication conditions, influences on each other, etc.) that are lurking beneath the surface (these discussions also often happen between people who feel at ease with each other, so it's hardly brought into the open for the entire workplace). **Things that aren't discussed are of course harder to see, so it's only natural that everyone will tend to focus on the work and problems that everyone shares, since they're easier to see.**

There is a scene in *The Little Prince* by Antoine de Saint-Exupéry with the following lines:

"Grown-ups like numbers. When you tell them about a new friend, they never ask questions about what really matters."

(In summary: They will ask questions about things like the friend's age and act as if they understand a person from that.)

"It is only with the heart that one can truly see that which is inevitably invisible to the eye."

◆ What Is Needed to See the Human Side?

When it comes to the human heart and the human side, lots of things are happening in the iceberg beneath the surface, **but you will never see any of it unless you go out of your way to try and see it.**

In order to see the obscure things that are going on within people's minds, you will have to start by talking to them and asking them to share their thoughts. By sharing your own thoughts as well, you can have an exchange like Sakigake and Hanami and discuss things from the perspective of the human side.

For Organization Development to progress, the most important attitude people must have is the attitude to try and see the obscure, human side of the workplace.

Heifetz states that seeing the true nature of what is happening before you and understanding this well is the most important key in solving adaptive challenges. Trying to see what exactly is happening before you and asking questions about it is the first step in improving a workplace or organization. It leads to the first of the three steps in Organization Development, seeing the problem.

3-2   The Core Team to Propel Change

◆ Propelling and Suppressing Change

When it comes to problems in workplaces and organizations, it's most often the case that there are both people who feel the need for change as well as those who don't.

It's also more often the case than not that the people who want change are the minority. In this kind of situation, the power that wants things to stay the same **(suppressing power)** is usually greater than or equal to the power that wants things to change **(propelling power).**

People don't change just because you tell them to change. Even when it's for improvement, as long as the person in question cannot find and be satisfied with the meaning of the change, they will only stop resisting on a surface level. They will continue to oppose this change within themselves and will not actually try to change from within.

In order to drive change in an organization or workplace, there is a need to increase the propulsion for this change (see Figure 3-1). By increasing the energy of the minority of those who want change and mobilizing the people who want things to stay the same, the propelling power toward change will slowly overpower the suppressing power, and then change can occur. When people believe that the problems in the workplace or organization are their own, they encourage others to improve things, which propels change forward.

◆ A Core Team to Increasingly Propel Change

Even if someone wants to change their workplace for the better, change cannot be propelled forward by one person alone. A **core team** is the **key to increasing the driving force toward change.** By building a core team of members who want change to happen, their energy will bounce off one another and increasingly propel change. A decision will have to be made regarding which members to put in the core team. The two things to focus on in building this core team are ① **increasing the propelling power for change** and ② **making the team a microcosm of the workplace or organization at large.**

① Increasing the Propelling Power for Change

You should choose people who aim for the same desirable outcome and will work to improve things (like Hirose and Hanami in the story).

These are the types of people to look for:
- People who are aware of the problems in the present situation

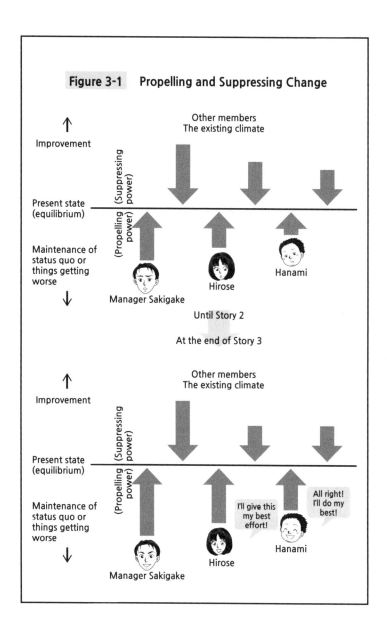

Figure 3-1   Propelling and Suppressing Change

- People who wish to better the organization or workplace
- People who show concern for other people and relationships—factors on the human side of the organization
- People who see others and cooperation (working as a team) as important

You should gather somewhat homogenous members who have similar aims and values.

② Making the Team a Microcosm of the Workplace or Organization at Large

This means that you should aim to build a team that's representative of the many different members in the workplace or organization. In other words, the team should be like a scaled-down version of the entire organization. You want to gather members who are different from one another. In the story, the member who represents this is Akemoto.

These are the types of people to look for:
- People who have different opinions and ideas (however, they must share the goal to improve the workplace)
- People who don't immediately conform with everyone else, people who think independently
- People with the authority to implement things

However, if the core team members' aims and values are too different from each others', someone will always be against proceeding with the project in the discussions, and this will suppress change instead of propelling it. In this case, the core team can't perform its function, and the Organization Development plans can't move forward, so caution is advised.

3-3 Propelling Organization Development

◆ Roles Needed Besides the Core Team

To improve an organization or workplace, there will be
other roles and functions needed besides the core team.
There's the **reform leader**, the **Organization Development
facilitator**, and the **sponsor**. Which person performs which
function is explained below.

◆ Transformation Leader

In this book, the reform leader in the story is the store
manager, Sakigake.

This person is the leader of the organization or the
workplace. The leader is the one who decides to carry
out Organization Development and the one who drives
the change. In a store, this would be the store manager;
in a department, the department chief; in a division, the
division chief; in a factory, the factory manager; and for the
whole company, this would be the CEO. The reform
leader is usually the top of whichever unit is going to
undergo Organization Development.

The role of the reform leader is to push the
implementation of Organization Development toward

Figure 3-2 **The Role of the Reform Leader**

WELL, I'VE BEEN OBSERVING YOU...

...AND YOU SEEM TO BE SOMEONE WHO CAN GET ALONG WITH OTHERS AND WORK WELL IN A TEAM.

- Driving the organization development efforts toward the desired outcome

- Implementing plans with the support of the Organization Development facilitator

- Talking to the members during discussions and implementing communication toward objectives and meaning (avoid giving orders and returning to previous conditions)

- Studying the situation along with the members and learning to realize things with them

- Encouraging the implementation of plans aiming at improving the situation

everyone's desired outcome. The reform leader discusses things with the Organization Development facilitator, who will be introduced in the next section. With the help of the facilitator, the reform leader implements the plans and strategies that have been discussed.

Before implementing any strategies or holding any discussions, the leader gathers the members and communicates the objective and the significance of their plans. During the actual discussion and implementation, the reform leader must also take care to avoid giving orders or controlling the situation and going back to the status quo. The reform leader goes through the three Organization Development steps—seeing the problem, serious discussion, and building a future—with the members (subordinates) to study the situation and learn to realize things with them.

Furthermore, the reform leader will support the members and encourage the continuation of the transformation in order to implement the plans and strategies decided in the "building a future" stage.

◆ Organization Development Supporter

In the story, the facilitator is Mizushina from the head office Organization Development team.

This role is usually filled in by someone in the company who understands Organization Development well, by a member of a division that specializes in Organization Development (from HR or from an Organization Development team), or an Organization Development consultant from another company. These people are not part of the unit that's the target of the development and **operates as a third-party supporter for the entire Organization Development process.**

The role of the facilitator isn't to lead the process but to guide the members on how to go about the entire thing. **They support the process and work alongside the members of the organization.**

Figure 3-3	The Role of the Organization Development Facilitator

- ° Supporting the implementation of Organization Development and working alongside the members

- ° In the beginning stages, explaining what Organization Development is and its objective, explaining the significance of looking into the human side of the organization

- ° Supporting and facilitating the members and the leader in the going through the process of Organization Development

The process by which the facilitator joins the effort and supports the organization members is called **process consultation** and is explained further on page 126.

◆ Sponsor

The Sponsor **understands the process of Organization Development and provides psychological and financial support** for the undertaking.

In Organization Development, the employees will have to spend time discussing issues, which will occasionally result in cases where a consultant from outside the company will need to be hired. These cases will incur an extra monetary expense for the company. The sponsor is the person with the power to decide whether or not to proceed with the

I...
DO?

Figure 3-4   The Role of the Sponsor

○ Understanding the objective, significance, desired outcome, and procedure of the Organization Development process that the workplace is undertaking

○ Supporting the Organization Development process psychologically and financially

○ Considering the cost and deciding to go through with the process (having the power to make that decision)

Organization Development process after considering the time and money it will cost.

In a division, the one who becomes the sponsor is the division chief. In a department, it's the head in charge of the department. In a company, this would be the CEO, president, or the head of HR.

If these people do not understand the Organization Development process, it will be very difficult to go through the process and see it through until the end. To that end, it is then necessary to properly explain to these people the objective and significance, the desired outcome, and the process of Organization Development.

There are also cases where the reform leader and the sponsor will be the same person. This person will then make the decision to spend time and money while also driving the process forward.

In the story, Sakigake is both the reform leader and the sponsor for their store.

3-4 Process Consultation—How Do Supporters Support Organization Development?

◆ The Three Styles of Support

In this section, we will shine a spotlight on and take a better look at Mizushina's role in the story. Mizushina plays the role of an internal company consultant, or facilitator, whose task is to support the Organization Development process.

In considering the role of an Organization Development facilitator, it's useful to look at the **three helping styles** proposed by Edgar Schein. Schein is famous for his research on Career Development and Organizational Culture, but he was originally (and still remains) a researcher of Organization Development. The three helping styles we're about to look at were proposed by him in 1969.

Schein stated that there are three styles of helping people and helping an organization change. These are **the expert style, the doctor-patient style, and the process consultation style.**

◆ The Specialist Style: Teaching Solution Strategies and Giving Information

In the expert style, an expert **gives information and teaches the members about solution strategies.** Examples would be if a company cannot design a personnel system for itself and hires a consultant to help, or when a company hires a system engineer to computerize their work system.

According to Schein, **this style is effective when people in a workplace or organization understand what their problem is and know that the solution offered by the consultant or facilitator will help them solve this problem.** Relating this to Heifetz's ideas, this style functions effectively when the problem the members are facing is a technical problem and the one helping them is an expert or authority in that field.

◆ Doctor-Patient Style: Diagnosis and Prescription

Just as you would ask a doctor to examine you, give results, and write you a prescription, in the doctor-patient style, **you ask the facilitator to gather data about the state of your organization or workplace (through a hearing or an assessment) and have them report the results.**

This style of support is effective when the members do not know what their current problem is. If the prescribed solution strategy can be implemented, then there is a possibility that this problem will be solved.

However, in most cases, the problem doesn't get solved in this manner. There are plenty of cases where an assessment is held and the results are reported to the organization or workplace superiors. However, these instances alone are never enough to solve the problem. One possible case is when **the prescribed solution doesn't get implemented successfully.** Another possible reason is that most of the problems on the human side of organizations and workplaces include adaptive challenges. These **cannot be solved by results, and solutions prescribed by an external source.**

To deal with problems that happen on the human side of an organization or workplace (adaptive challenges), the members of that group will need to hold a discussion to study the problem, establish what the fundamental problem is, come up with a solution, and implement it themselves. Supporting this kind of process is what the process consultation style is all about.

◆ Process Consultation Style: Participatory Support

The process consultation style is different from having an expert provide the solution (expert style) or from having someone assess the situation and prescribe a solution (doctor-patient style). Let's take a look at how they differ by considering the example of a middle-aged man who has been having weight issues.

The expert style in this situation would involve joining a diet program and following the orders of an expert trainer.

There's a possibility that the man succeeds with his diet, but he might also rebound after the program is over.

	Description	Situations Where the Style Is Effective
Figure 3-5		The Three Helping Styles
The Expert Style	The helper gives information and solutions.	The people in a workplace or organization understand what their problem is and know that the solution offered by the consultant or facilitator will help them solve this problem.
The Doctor-Patient Style	The helper gives a diagnosis and prescription.	The people concerned do not know what the problem is yet and need to wait for a diagnosis before implementing a solution.
The Process Consultation Style	The helper supports the members as a companion.	The people concerned have realized what the problem is and need to come up with and implement a solution themselves (adaptive challenge).

In a doctor-patient style, the overweight man would go to the doctor for an examination and listen to the advice of the doctor. While this helps him understand the state his body is in, he might say yes to the doctor's orders (like cutting back on food or exercising) on the spot but then fail to actually follow their advice.

For the process consultation style, the helper encourages the overweight man to **realize the problem, plan a**

solution, and implement it himself. This style is similar to coaching or counseling.

In Organization Development, the consultant facilitates and supports the process so that the people concerned can go through the steps (seeing the problem, serious discussion, and building a future) themselves.

◆ An Example of Process Consultation Support

Let's look at the process consultation style in more detail by considering the story in this book.

First, Mizushina helped the people in the branch in seeing the problem. As a third party, she held the hearing, organized the data they obtained, and reported the results as a means to start a discussion among the members. After that, during the feedback meeting (the "seeing the problem" step) in Story 2, she tries to push the members to express their views and feelings (facilitation), interfering as little as possible.

During the discussion of the core team in Story 3, Hirose asks her what they need to do. She tells her that neither she nor the store manager will give them any orders, and the members will have to decide among themselves. If she gave them orders here, she would have switched to the expert style of helping. Instead, by not giving orders, she was able to convey the importance of the core members identifying the problem and discussing what they'll do by themselves.

It might be easier to visualize what the process consultation style is like by revisiting Story 2 and Story 3 and focusing on Mizushina's actions.

The people concerned are the ones who will have to deal with the obscure problems found on the human side of an organization. The Organization Development facilitator will provide the support to keep the process moving forward. This method of doing things in the process consultation style was also reflected in the story.

◆ **Building a Support Relationship as a Participant**

Most of the problems on the human side of organizations are adaptive challenges, and the people concerned will have to study them through discussion to deal with them by themselves. **Engaging in this process _as a participant_** is the process consultation style of helping.

It might be easier to visualize what the process consultation style is like by revisiting Story 2 and Story 3 and focusing on Mizushina's actions.

According to Schein, the most important thing in this style of helping is to **build a support relationship** with the members. The point is to avoid building a relationship where the facilitator points out what to do or does it themselves, which is what happens in normal consultation processes. Building a support relationship begins with making sure that the members understand the Organization Development facilitator's role. Their role is at times to gather data and to be someone who drives the discussion while moving alongside the members. Then as the members realize the problem, to plan a solution and implement it. Building this relationship is the foundation of progress in Organization Development.

Part 3

From Individual Work to Cooperation

STORY 4
TOWARD BEING ABLE TO TEACH EACH OTHER

CORE TEAM MEETING

AKEMOTO-SAN TOLD ME THAT HIS BUSINESS MEETING IS GOING ON LONGER THAN EXPECTED, SO HE'LL BE LATE.

ALL RIGHT. WE DON'T HAVE MUCH TIME THOUGH, SO LET'S START WITHOUT HIM.

UMM...

PLEASE DON'T GET ME WRONG! I DO WANT TO DO THINGS.

ABOUT THE CORE TEAM...

RIGHT NOW, I HAVE ABSOLUTELY NO IDEA WHAT WE'RE SUPPOSED TO ACTUALLY DO AND HOW.

INSTEAD OF THINKING ABOUT WHAT TO DO AND HOW...

...WHY DON'T WE FIRST TRY TO THINK ABOUT WHAT PROBLEMS NEED SOLVING?

SORRY?

LET'S TAKE THE PROBLEMS THAT WERE BROUGHT UP IN THE FEEDBACK MEETING A FEW DAYS BACK, FOR EXAMPLE.

WHICH AMONG THOSE WOULD YOU SAY YOU AGREE WITH THE LEAST?

HMMM...

THE IDEA THAT THE MORNING MEETINGS AND SHARING OPINIONS IS A WASTE OF TIME.

ON THE CONTRARY, THEN, WHY DO YOU THINK THOSE ARE NECESSARY?

I WANT TO LEARN FROM THE OTHER EMPLOYEES! THERE'S STILL SO MUCH I DON'T KNOW.

OH, BUT...

BUT?

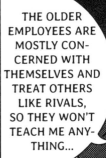

THE OLDER EMPLOYEES ARE MOSTLY CONCERNED WITH THEMSELVES AND TREAT OTHERS LIKE RIVALS, SO THEY WON'T TEACH ME ANYTHING...

IT DOESN'T FEEL LIKE WE'RE PART OF THE SAME TEAM AT ALL.

I-IF I MAY...

THEY ALSO DIDN'T TEACH ME MUCH.

YOU NEED TO LEARN THE ROPES OF SALES WORK YOURSELF.

YOU EARN SALES WITH LEGWORK, SO JUST HURRY UP AND GET OUT THERE.

THERE'S VERY LITTLE TEACHING AND COOPERATION.

I SUPPOSE EMPLOYEES HERE HAVE REALLY TURNED TO DOING WORK ON THEIR OWN.

NOW THAT YOU MENTION IT, THAT IS WHAT'S BEEN HAPPENING...

IF WE TALKED ABOUT AIMING TO BUILD MORE CO-OPERATIVE WORK RELATIONSHIPS WHERE EVERYONE TEACHES EACH OTHER...

...THEN MAYBE NO ONE WILL THINK THAT THE MORNING MEETINGS ARE A WASTE OF TIME!

I LIKE THAT! MAYBE ONE-MINUTE SPEECHES IN THE MORNINGS COULD WORK?

THAT SOUNDS GREAT!

LET'S ASK EVERYONE TO SHARE ANY TIPS OR EXPERIENCES THEY HAVE ABOUT SALES!

137

I'M BACK.

OH, HELLO.

HOPE THE MEETING WENT WELL!

RIGHT NOW, WE'RE CONSIDERING THE IDEA OF HAVING ONE-MINUTE SPEECHES IN THE MORNING TO SHARE TIPS ABOUT SALES WORK.

...

I DON'T THINK IT WOULD WORK, BUT YOU CAN GO AHEAD AND TRY.

ALL RIGHT!

MORNING MEETINGS? WE'RE DO-ING THOSE AGAIN?

YES!

WE'RE ALSO THINKING OF HAVING PEOPLE DO ONE-MINUTE SPEECHES...

WHAT DO WE EVEN TALK ABOUT?

WELL... YOU COULD GIVE US TIPS ABOUT SALES WORK.

HUH?

WHY WOULD I SHARE THAT WITH ANYONE?

RIGHT NOW? I'M BUSY.

UMM, WE'RE THINKING OF HOLDING MORNING MEETINGS AGAIN. WOULD YOU BE WILLING TO MAKE A SHORT SPEECH ABOUT YOUR SALES EXPERIENCES?

SUGOI CAR CATALOG

IN FRONT OF EVERYONE? NO, I DON'T THINK SO.

GLOOMY

I COULDN'T CONVINCE ANYONE.

OH. WELL, LET ME TRY AND ASK OTHER PEOPLE AS WELL.

HAN-AMI!

COPY THIS FOR ME.

OKAY.

WHIRR

SMILE SMILE

...

DID YOU GET A THANK-YOU LETTER FROM A CLIENT? THAT'S GREAT!

RIGHT? THEY SAID SOME REALLY NICE THINGS TOO.

OHH!

WANNA HEAR THE STORY?

VERY MUCH!

THE STORY STARTS A FEW MONTHS AGO.

I'VE BEEN THINKING OF REPLACING OUR CAR WITH A STATION WAGON.

WELL ...

IS THAT SO? IN THAT CASE...

ACTUALLY, EVER SINCE MY FATHER WAS CONFINED TO A WHEELCHAIR...

... HE'S BEEN HESITANT ABOUT GOING OUT.

HE'S AGAINST BUYING A NEW CAR. HE SAYS WE DON'T HAVE TO DO THAT JUST FOR HIM.

BUT I'VE BEEN DREAMING OF GOING OUT TOGETHER AS A FAMILY AGAIN...

I SEE.

SNUB

WILL YOU LET ME HELP YOU FULFILL THAT DREAM?

HUH?

IT'S BEEN MY DREAM TO FULFILL A CLIENT'S DREAM!

WILL YOU LET ME HELP FULFILL YOURS?

ALL RIGHT. PLEASE HELP ME FIND THE RIGHT CAR.

I THOUGHT ABOUT WHAT I CAN DO FOR THEM.

TO MAKE THE NEW CAR EASY TO DRIVE NOT JUST FOR HIM BUT ALSO FOR HIS WIFE...

...I OFFERED TO LET THEM TEST DRIVE A CAR WITH A REAR-VIEW MONI-TOR.

143

AND THE GRANDFATHER'S FEELINGS ALSO STARTED TO CHANGE.

GRANDPA!

LET'S GO OUT TOGETHER IN THE NEW CAR!

WELL, I GUESS IT WOULDN'T HURT.

EXCITED

AND THEN? WHAT HAPPENED AFTER THAT?

THEY ENDED UP BUYING THE CAR.

THEY SENT ME THIS PHOTO WITH THEIR LETTER.

THAT'S SUCH A NICE STORY!

TOUCHED

AREN'T YOU GETTING A BIT TOO EMOTIONAL?

DOING SALES IS A WONDERFUL JOB, ISN'T IT?

THAT'S RIGHT! I MEAN, IT'S A BUSY JOB WITH LOTS OF DIFFICULTIES...

...BUT A GRATEFUL CLIENT LIKE THIS MAKES IT ALL WORTH IT!

145

THE DAY MORNING MEETINGS RESUMED.

A FEW DAYS AGO, SUZUKI-SENPAI RECEIVED A THANK-YOU LETTER, AND I WAS VERY TOUCHED BY THE STORY!

I'M SURE EVERYONE WOULD BE GLAD TO HEAR THE STORY TOO! WOULD YOU LIKE TO SHARE IT HERE?

WHA?! YOU...

I'D VERY MUCH LIKE TO HEAR ABOUT IT TOO! PLEASE TELL US.

A-ALL RIGHT. WELL...

THAT'S A NICE STORY.

SOMETHING SIMILAR HAPPENED TO ME.

KINDA TOUCHING.

AFTER THE MEETING...

SEN-PAI!

I'M REALLY SORRY FOR SUDDENLY ASKING YOU TO TALK EARLIER.

YEAH! YOU REALLY PUT ME ON THE SPOT THERE!

BUT EVERYONE WAS MOVED BY YOUR STORY!

R-REALLY?

WHAT DO YOU THINK CONVINCED THE CLIENT TO TRUST YOU?

WELL, IF I HAD TO SAY...

...INSTEAD OF TELLING YOUR CLIENT YOU'LL FULFILL THEIR DREAM...

...YOU TELL THEM THAT IT'S YOUR DREAM TO FULFILL THEIR DREAM.

DURING ANOTHER MORNING MEETING...

I WAS REALLY MOVED BY SUZUKI-SENPAI'S STORY A FEW DAYS AGO, SO I TRIED HIS APPROACH, AND IT WORKED!

WOW! CONGRATULATIONS!

CLAP CLAP CLAP

IT WASN'T A HUGE SALE THOUGH...

LAU-GH

PLEASE LET ME TRY...

...YOUR WAY TOO, SUZUKI-SENPAI!

WHA?

PLEASE!

I ALSO WANT TO KNOW HOW YOU DID IT!

OH, WELL, WHY NOT? SO, THE THING IS, IT'S NOT ABOUT FULFILLING YOUR CLIENT'S DREAMS...

THANKS TO HANAMI-SAN, WE'VE FOUND AN APPROACH FOR BUILDING RELATIONSHIPS WHERE EVERY-ONE TEACHES EACH OTHER.

IT WAS REALLY BY CHANCE. I WAS JUST HONESTLY CURIOUS ABOUT THE THANK-YOU LETTER.

THATMEANS THAT YOU WERE UNCONSCIOUSLY ABLE TO ENCOURAGE EVERYONE TO MOVE AWAY FROM DOING WORK JUST BY THEMSELVES.

I EN-COUR-AGED PEO-PLE...

149

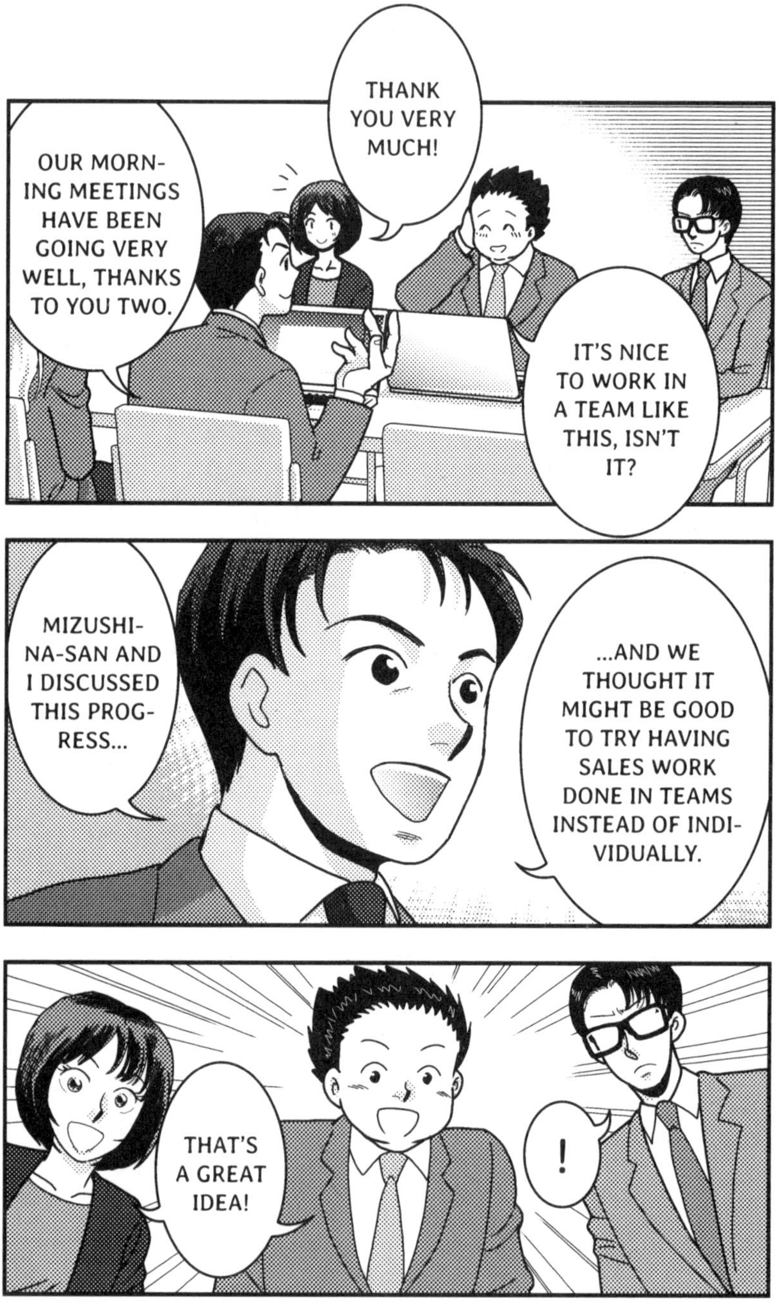
OUR MORNING MEETINGS HAVE BEEN GOING VERY WELL, THANKS TO YOU TWO.
THANK YOU VERY MUCH!
IT'S NICE TO WORK IN A TEAM LIKE THIS, ISN'T IT?
MIZUSHINA-SAN AND I DISCUSSED THIS PROGRESS...
...AND WE THOUGHT IT MIGHT BE GOOD TO TRY HAVING SALES WORK DONE IN TEAMS INSTEAD OF INDIVIDUALLY.
THAT'S A GREAT IDEA!
!

IN A LATER MORNING MEETING...

WE WANT TO INTRODUCE A MORE COOPERATIVE WAY OF DOING SALES, SO WE'RE CONSIDERING TURNING SALES INTO A TEAM EFFORT.

WE'LL FIRST TRY IT WITH A PILOT TEAM OF SORTS AND GO FROM THERE.

GASP

WHAT?

WHISPER

WHISPER

ARE THEY TRYING SOMETHING NEW AGAIN?

SOUNDS GOOD THOUGH, DOESN'T IT?

WHISPER

MUTTER

IF WE GET BETTER RESULTS THAN BY WORKING INDIVIDUALLY, THEN I'M ALL FOR IT.

MUTTER

AND SO, THE TEAM SALES (TRIAL RUN) BEGAN.

ALL RIGHT! LET'S GO SELL SOME CARS!

YES!

MY NEGO- TIATION DIDN'T GO WELL ...

CAN YOU TELL US WHAT YOU DID?

IT'LL WORK OUT NEXT TIME!

ONE WEEK AF- TER...

GOOD JOB!

I CLOSED THE SALE!

CON- GRATS!

CLA- TTER

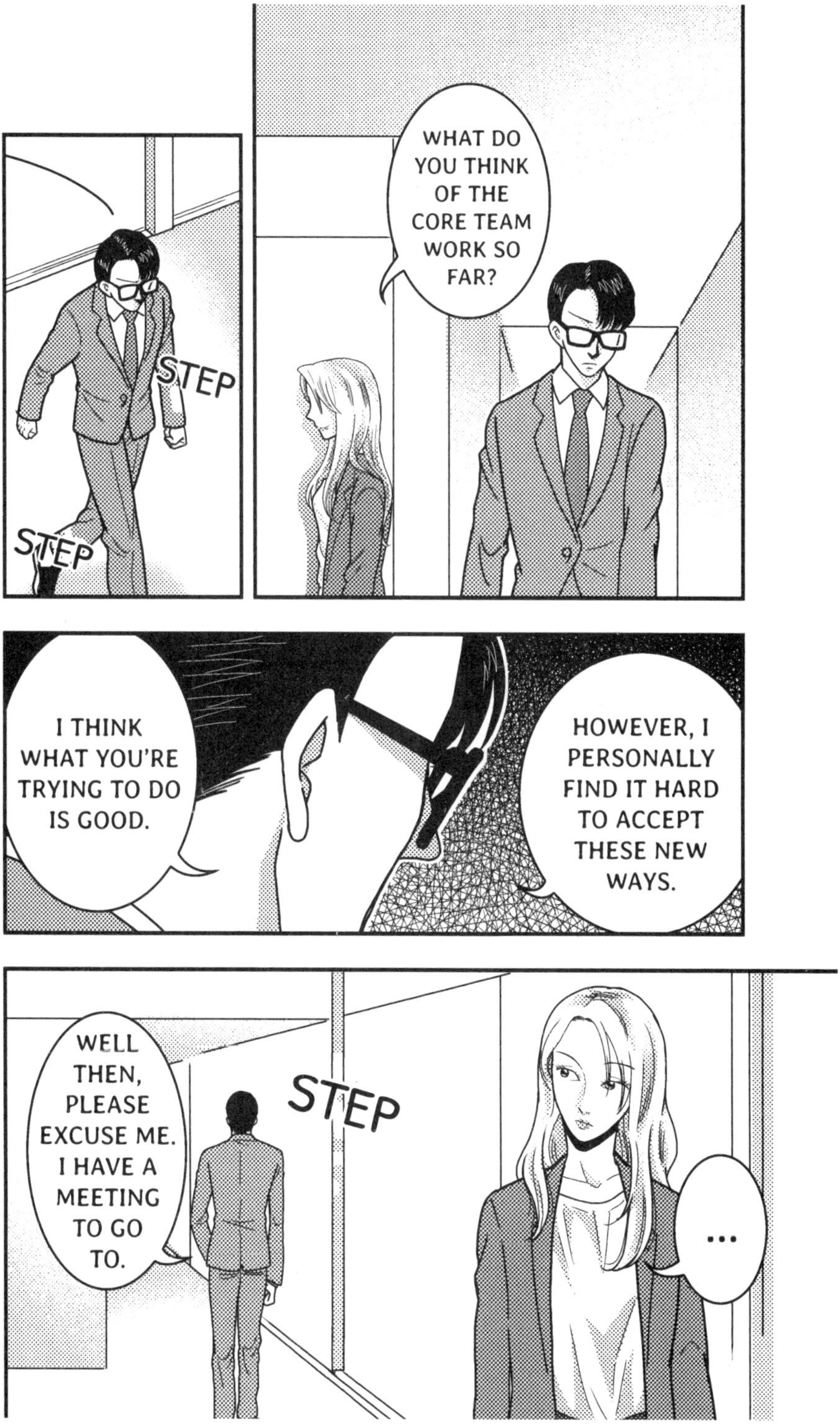
STEP
STEP
WHAT DO YOU THINK OF THE CORE TEAM WORK SO FAR?
I THINK WHAT YOU'RE TRYING TO DO IS GOOD.
HOWEVER, I PERSONALLY FIND IT HARD TO ACCEPT THESE NEW WAYS.
WELL THEN, PLEASE EXCUSE ME. I HAVE A MEETING TO GO TO.
STEP
...

Through discussion, the core team found and confirmed that the fundamental problem was the **individual work style** of the store. This stage is part of the serious discussion step in Organization Development.

After this, Hirose said that she wanted a more cooperative work environment where everyone can teach each other. To achieve this, she comes up with the idea of resuming the morning meetings, and they implement this idea. Here, they plan their approach and implement it in order to realize their desired outcome. This is the **"building a future"** stage.

After resuming the morning meetings with a new objective in mind, Hirose and Hanami, from the core team, then try to encourage and convince other employees in the store. We can see that their drive is high as they move toward their desired outcome of having a work environment where everyone can teach one another.

However, this individual work style has become the norm in the store, and they encounter resistance from the employees who see this style as the standard. Other employees' responses to Hirose include comments such as how they cannot share their sales knowledge and how it's impossible for them to make a speech in front of everyone.

This attitude and behavior where people want to remain the same is called **resistance to change**. Whenever someone aims to change the present climate or relationships in an organization, they are bound to always encounter this resistance to change.

Hanami happened to see one of his senior co-workers smiling while reading a thank-you letter from a client. This gave Hanami a chance to learn about his co-worker's success story and what he values in his work. Hanami then encouraged this co-worker to share his story during one of their newly revived morning meetings. The co-worker was embarrassed and hesitated at first but ultimately shared the story. This new connection becomes a small success, and people start to take the morning meetings as a place to foster teaching and making connections, instead of just a waste of time. We then see a slow decline in resistance against the morning meetings.

The individual approach to work seen in this book's story isn't unique to that store. This can be seen in many companies

Through Hanami's efforts, the employees started to move from working individually to having teaching and learning relationships (cooperation) with others in the office.

and organizations all throughout the world. As stated in the introduction of this book, this individual approach to work is also one of the reasons why Organization Development is in demand.

That is why in this part, we will first look at **why individual work has become widespread.** Through Hanami's efforts, the employees started to move from working individually to having teaching and learning relationships (cooperation) with others in the office and to the problems associated with it. We will also look at what's needed to move from individual to cooperative work.

Next, we will tackle the resistance to change that can be observed when Organization Development strategies are implemented and how to handle this resistance. We will also look at the importance of garnering small successes in order to move toward everyone's desired outcome.

Through the accumulation of small successes, the workplace in the story started to change little by little.

4-1 Moving from Individual Work to Cooperation

◆ Why Work Is Being Done Individually

The individual approach to work can be seen in many different industries. In sales, each employee is assigned their own clients or areas, and they deal with them on their own. In planning and development, the parts and portions of the product being developed are distributed to different employees, and each one works on the part they've been assigned to. In manufacturing factories, each person has a process or machine assigned to them, and they monitor these and deal with any trouble that arises on their own.

The common factor here is that our current approach to work basically consists of dividing the whole into parts and assigning each part to an individual. That is, we've come to prefer **division of labor**. The tendency to deal with assigned work on one's own is the **individual approach to work**.

Until around the 1980s, teamwork was deemed to be a strong point in Japanese industries. American culture, on the other hand, is founded on individualism People discussed how to improve their product in Quality Control Circles. They tried to increase productivity in small groups and exchanged ideas in informal discussions. American culture, on the other hand, is based on individualism, but many American companies have incorporated Quality Control Circles and the related concept of Kaizen groups to improve safety and health, product design, and manufacturing processes.

In Japan, approaching work cooperatively in teams and workplaces was the norm back then.

However, division of labor and approaching work individually are the norm nowadays.

The following are possible reasons why the individual approach is preferred.

- With the advent of computers and automation, there is now a lot more work that can be done individually.
- Work has become more specialized, and there's more work that requires knowledge and information that only the person assigned understands.
- Work has become more busy, and with the focus on efficiency and constraint on overtime work, meetings and discussions have become shorter.
- It has become the norm to deal with one's assigned work alone.

It's believed that this individual approach to work will only become more widespread with the work-style reform and increase in remote work.

◆ The Shortcomings of Individual Work

People will need to invest time for communication in order to discuss things as a team and cooperate with one another.

With many companies reducing their meeting times, one of the advantages of approaching work individually is the reduction of this kind of communication cost (the work and time put into conversation). Another advantage is that it allows an individual to exhibit their full potential (they are not constrained by others).

Of course, individual work also has disadvantages: ① It cannot make use of team synergy. ② It does not give people the chance to build trust and supportive relationships with one another. ③ It can lead to a decline in team strength (people become more concerned with themselves and less concerned about others and the team). ④ There is stress and mental health issues that stem from having to do work on one's own. ⑤ It doesn't give people the chance to teach each other and learn together. ⑥ As a result, long-term personnel training becomes difficult.

As stated above, one of the advantages of individual work is the reduction of communication cost, that is, less input is needed. On the other hand, cooperative work can increase team synergy and there's a possibility for innovation. This can increase long-term outputs such as team improvement and personnel training.

In short, it becomes important to decide what you want to aim for in order to increase productivity (decrease the input or increase the output).

Figure 4-1	The Advantages and Disadvantages of Individual Work

Advantages

• Lower communication cost (less input)

• Can work at own discretion, so individuals can exhibit their full potential (they are not constrained by others)

Disadvantages

• Less concerned about others and the team

• Stress and mental health issues that stem from having to do work on your own

• Cannot teach each other and learn together

• As a result, long-term personnel training becomes difficult

◆ **From Individual to Cooperative Work**

Individual work has now become the norm and will probably only get more widespread from here on. If nothing is done about this tendency toward individual work, the shortcomings associated with it listed in the previous page will keep expanding. This will undoubtedly harm people's natural ability to cooperate in teams. **In order to move from individual to cooperative work, there is a need to employ intrinsic strategy and purposefully steer away from the current trend.**

When individual work is already ingrained into the company culture, it becomes harder to change this practice. However, the primary points to focus on in order to move from individual to cooperative work at the workplace level are actually quite simple. First, you will need to **establish a place or structure where multiple people can have a discussion, cooperate, and learn together.** The other is **to have the members of the workplace share the meaning and significance of moving to cooperative work** (however, as always, these things are easier said than done, so be sure to take them simply as points to focus on).

Some examples of the first point found in the story are making sales teams; establishing a place where people can share their experiences and learn from each other (like the morning meetings); establishing places and structures where people can give feedback to each other; and discussing, planning, and implementing plans regarding work-style reform and work improvement as a team.

However, as seen in Part 1, **merely applying these techniques won't lead to the desired results.** In the case of sales, establishing sales teams would be a solution strategy for a technical problem, and the chances that this alone will lead to the change from individual to cooperative work is low. It's important for the members to go through the process of the three steps—seeing the problem, serious discussion, and building a future—and study the prevalence of individual work at their workplace in order to change how they perceive (learning) the current situation.

Shown in Figure 4-2 are the important points to remember when trying to move from individual to cooperative work.

So far, we've been looking at the process of moving from individual to cooperative work. In the next section, the topic will be slightly different. We will be taking a look at the process of expanding Organization Development.

In the story, the workplace also changed because the core team went through the three-step process of seeing the problem, serious discussion, and building a future.

Figure 4-2   Moving from Individual to Cooperative Work

(Premise)

If most members consider individual work to be the norm, change
will not happen.

Go through the three steps—seeing the problem, serious discussion, and
building a future—regarding individual work (establish what the problem with
individual work is and what kind of outcome to aim for).

In addition, regularly set up a place for discussion toward
cooperation and make plans together.

4-2 Expanding Organization Development

◆ Structured and Unstructured Organization Development

One side of Organization Development involves preparing a place for discussion where everyone gathers and talks things out (just like the feedback meeting in Story 1). Another side of it involves using everyday connections and encouragement to drive progress (like how Hirose and Hanami went around trying to convince their senior co-workers in Story 4). The first side is termed **structured Organization Development** and the second is **unstructured Organization Development connection and approach.**

Most people's idea of Organization Development probably involves gathering people and having a discussion to implement techniques using a ton of unknown jargon. There are also people practicing Organization Development who equate it to implementing methods and techniques under it. In short, people think that Organization Development involves only structured things. However, this is a **narrow way of viewing Organization Development.**

Using only structured techniques like the feedback meeting in Story 2 usually isn't enough to spark change in an organization or workplace. By going through the three steps—seeing the problem, serious discussion, and building a future—in a structured place for discussion, the plans and actions agreed upon in the "building a future" step are executed on a daily basis, and only then does change actually start. This means that the structured place for discussion is only the start. What's more crucial are the unstructured Organization Development connections and approaches found in everyday life.

There is also an approach where the Organization Development consultant (Organization Development facilitator) regularly joins the company meetings and tries to work on the human side issues that arise then and there. This is one of the forms of the process consultation style mentioned before and falls under unstructured Organization Development.

◆ Increasing the Power of the Core Team to Transform Itself

One of the definitions of Organization Development discussed earlier included improving the workplace or organization's effectiveness, health, and ability to self-innovate. Organization Development looks at the human side of organizations and workplaces with the aim to improve it, but **what's especially important is improving the ability of the people in that organization or workplace to *self-innovate.***

Self-innovation includes the word "self," which refers to the individual and can be taken to mean **the power of individuals to change themselves.** In Organization Development, the members realize what the problem is and work on improving it themselves. In this context, self-innovation means the ability of a team, workplace, or organization to continuously innovate and learn. It's **the power to continuously solve the obscure problems that arise on the human side of organizations and keep improving.** Self-innovation is, in this sense, **the ability to continuously go through the three-step process of seeing the problem, having serious discussion, and building a future.**

Ultimately, you want to improve self-innovation in the entire workplace or organization, but this kind of improvement doesn't just suddenly happen. First, you have to start with the core team.

If you've assembled a core team to drive the progress of Organization Development in your workplace, the core team members will first realize what the problem is by themselves and approach the other members to persuade

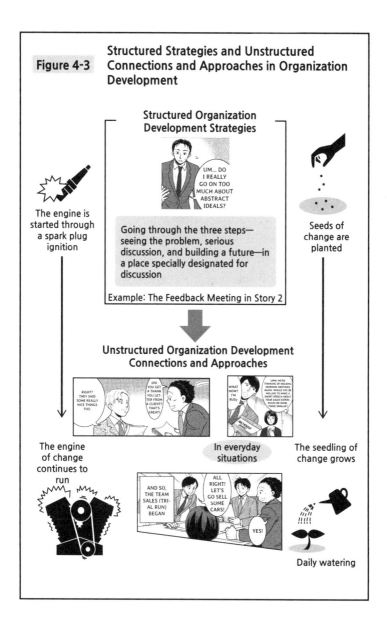

Figure 4-3 Structured Strategies and Unstructured Connections and Approaches in Organization Development

Structured Organization Development Strategies

UM... DO I REALLY GO ON TOO MUCH ABOUT ABSTRACT IDEALS?

Going through the three steps—seeing the problem, serious discussion, and building a future—in a place specially designated for discussion

Example: The Feedback Meeting in Story 2

The engine is started through a spark plug ignition

Seeds of change are planted

Unstructured Organization Development Connections and Approaches

RIGHT? THEY SAID SOME REALLY NICE THINGS TOO.

DID YOU GET A THANK YOU LETTER FROM A CLIENT? THAT'S GREAT!

WHAT NOW? I'M BUSY

UHM, WE'RE THINKING OF HOLDING MORNING MEETINGS AGAIN, WOULD YOU BE WILLING TO MAKE A SHORT SPEECH ABOUT YOUR SALES EXPERIENCES OR SOMETHING SIMILAR?

The engine of change continues to run

In everyday situations

The seedling of change grows

AND SO, THE TEAM SALES (TRIAL RUN) BEGAN

ALL RIGHT! LET'S GO SELL SOME CARS!

YES!

Daily watering

them. This is how self-innovation is improved starting with the core team. This kind of persuasion usually happens in everyday situations (like Hirose and Hanami's efforts in Story 4).

It would be difficult to improve self-innovation with only structured Organization Development. In structured approaches (the feedback meeting, for example) people will go through the three steps of Organization Development once, but it doesn't improve their ability to go through these steps by themselves. There is a need for the members to develop the habit of studying the current situation together through discussion in everyday work. This means that people will have to use **unstructured Organization Development approaches and go through small cycles of the three steps over and over again in their everyday work.** Through this, the workplace or organization, along with its ability to self-innovate, will keep improving.

Considering this, it can also be said that implementing structured strategies alone cannot be called Organization Development.

4-3　Dealing with Resistance to Change

◆ Resistance to Change Is Healthy

Whenever an organization or workplace decides to
implement Organization Development, having discussions
and new plans will usually see some negative reactions.
People will tend to ask if there's really any point to it
all and will say that they're too busy and don't have the
energy to spend on these projects. How to face this kind
of resistance to change is also a very important point to
consider for those who will be pushing for Organization
Development.

First, we need to understand that **resistance to
change** (expression of negative reactions toward new
undertakings) **is natural and is a sign of good health for
an organization.**

In the prologue, Sakigake was assigned as the new store
manager. When he started implementing new things
like the morning meetings, no one expressed their
dissatisfaction and complained. In that kind of situation,
dissatisfaction and negative reactions were brewing
within the employees, but they chose not to express
these opinions so no discussion can happen (they are at
the **polite discussion** level where there's only one-sided

communication or where people do not express their true opinions even when they show their reactions).

As discussed in Part 1, people give their own meanings to various happenings around them. Without a discussion, the negative meanings employees attach to new undertakings (there's no point or they don't have the time and energy to spare) cannot change. These meanings then stay negative. Changes undertaken that are wrapped in the employees' feelings of being forced cannot bring about positive change. **In implementing new changes and approaches, the most undesirable situation is one where the resistance to this change, dissatisfaction, complaints, and negative reactions are not brought to the surface.**

In line with this, in Story 4, when the core team members (Hirose and Hanami) reached out to other employees to aim for a work environment where everybody can teach one another, the employees expressed their opposition to the idea. One possible reason for this is that it was easier to express their disagreement since the members approaching

When Sakigake implemented the morning meetings in Story 1, the employees did not express any criticism or opposition.

170

them were younger. Nevertheless, it was still a good sign. It meant that they had moved from the polite discussion level to the **debate** level where people can express their straightforward opinions and honest thoughts.

Moving up further to the introspective discussion level also means progress for the Organization Development process.

◆ Dealing with Negative Reactions

Moving on, in this section, we will be looking at a couple of things to keep in mind when dealing with the people who are reacting negatively toward new approaches or plans.

First, you must take this to mean that they are **looking at something different or that they have a different way of perceiving things.** In Story 4, Hirose and Hanami asked their senior co-workers to share sales tips or stories about their work experiences during the morning meetings. The two of them perceived this action positively as a way to escape the dominance of individual work in the office and move toward a work environment where people can teach each other. However, their senior co-workers perceived this negatively, thinking it was just a waste of time. They thought there was no point in teaching each other, and they didn't want to do it. **This isn't about which view is right but rather about how people can perceive things differently.**

Discussions are needed in order to change people's perceptions. Hirose merely asked her senior co-workers to talk about their experiences or give some sales tips during the morning meetings. That is, she was not able to convey the meaning of these actions. If she were able to convey what was going on and able to express what her aim was and the significance in these actions, if she were able to attempt a discussion that could have changed her senior co-workers' perceptions, then she might have seen different results.

However, this doesn't mean that a discussion can change everyone's perceptions and make resistance go away. That's because **people will not be convinced of the meaning of doing something unless they experience it for themselves.** The next important thing to make progress in Organization Development is to **make small attempts (trials).**

◆ Building Successful Experiences through Small Attempts

In Story 4, Hanami approaches one of their senior co-workers, and this co-worker shares one of his successful experiences. The other employees listening to this felt moved, and some expressed that they experienced something similar. With these positive responses, everyone started to feel that there may be a point to sharing these success stories during the morning meetings. This kind of development is quite common. People experience

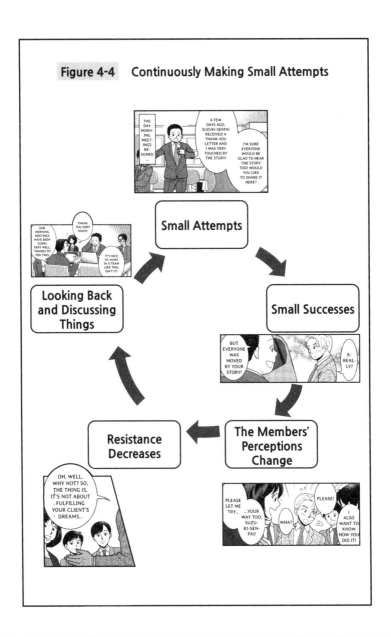

Figure 4-4   Continuously Making Small Attempts

something for themselves, and each person's perception turns into something positive.

In the latter part of Story 4, the department also decided to introduce a pilot sales team. This process also involves first making a small attempt through the pilot team instead of immediately implementing the team sales structure in the entire department.

If the reform leader or the core team decides to implement a big change, the other members' resistance will also be big. First, the core team should make small attempts and have the members experience them. Through this, the members' perception will change slightly (the members' resistance decreases), the supporters of change will increase, after which the core team can then make their next attempt. The point is to attempt things in small steps. Of course, it's also important to look back on these attempts and discuss them. By reflecting on and discussing their experiences together, the members are able to share their realizations and what they learned and collaborative learning becomes possible.

In the story, they were able to gradually build a work environment where people can teach each other through small attempts.

Part 4

Changing the Individual Mindset

STORY 5
Outgrowing Focus on Individual Work and Achievements

ALL RIGHT. I'M PLACING AN ORDER FOR FORTY UNITS.

IN THAT CASE, I'LL BRING OVER THE CONTRACT NEXT WEEK.

YES, PLEASE. I CAN REST EASY KNOWING YOU'LL BE TAKING CARE OF IT.

IF THIS CONTRACT GOES THROUGH, WE'RE GUARANTEED TO REACH THIS TERM'S TARGET!

I'M BACK.

CLATTER

ALL RIGHT, THEN. CAN YOU SHARE THE INFORMATION YOU GATHERED FROM YOUR MEETING?

YAMASHITA-SAN SAID THAT TAKING INTO CONSIDERATION GAS MILEAGE, HE'D LIKE TO BUY NEW CARS...

...BUT HE'S UNCERTAIN ABOUT HOW TO OPERATE NEWER VEHICLES.

KAWADA-SAMA SAYS SHE WILL DO HER INSPECTION AT A CHEAPER PLACE.

I SEE.

IN THESE CASES, YOU SHOULD TRY TO SYMPATHIZE WITH THE CUSTOMER...

EXPLAIN TO THEM WHAT GETTING A CHEAPER INSPECTION WOULD MEAN ...

RIGHT! THAT'S A POSSIBILITY TOO!

CLICK CLACK

177

BAR

WHAT'S THE POINT OF DOING SALES WORK THAT DOESN'T IN-CREASE SALES?

STEP
STEP
STEP

I'M NOT THEM, AND THEY'RE NOT ME. I SHOULD FOCUS ON MY OWN WORK. THAT'S ALL.

AH!
SLIDE

CRASH
EEEK!!
WAH!!

WEEEEOOO WEEEEOOO

THE NEXT DAY

AKE-MOTO-SAN!

...

I HEARD YOU BROKE BOTH OF YOUR LEGS. HOW ARE YOU DOING?

HERE'S MY DOCTOR'S NOTE.

I'M GLAD YOU WEREN'T SERIOUSLY HURT.

WE'LL TAKE CARE OF YOUR WORK, SO DON'T WORRY AND REST UP.

179

NO, THERE'S NO NEED FOR THAT.

BUT ...

IT'S FINE. I'LL DO IT ON MY OWN AS I ALWAYS HAVE.

ANY FURTHER VISITS ARE ALSO UNNECESSARY.

I UNDERSTAND. WELL, PLEASE DON'T HESITATE TO CONTACT ME IF YOU NEED ANYTHING.

AKEMO-TO-SAN! CALLS ARE PROHIBITED IN THE HOSPITAL!

APOLOGIES.

DAMN IT! I CAN'T MEET THE TARGET IF I LOSE THIS CONTRACT!

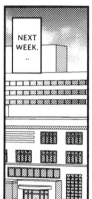

NEXT WEEK...

AKEMOTO-SAN, HOW ARE YOU DOING? ARE YO-

I SAID THERE'S NO NEED TO VISIT ME, DIDN'T I?

I HAVE A REPORT FOR YOU TODAY.

TWITCH

ABOUT YOUR CLIENTS...

...WE'VE RE-DISTRIBUTED THEM AND ARE MAKING PROGRESS.

YOU HAD A CONTRACT SCHEDULED FOR THIS WEEK, RIGHT?

182

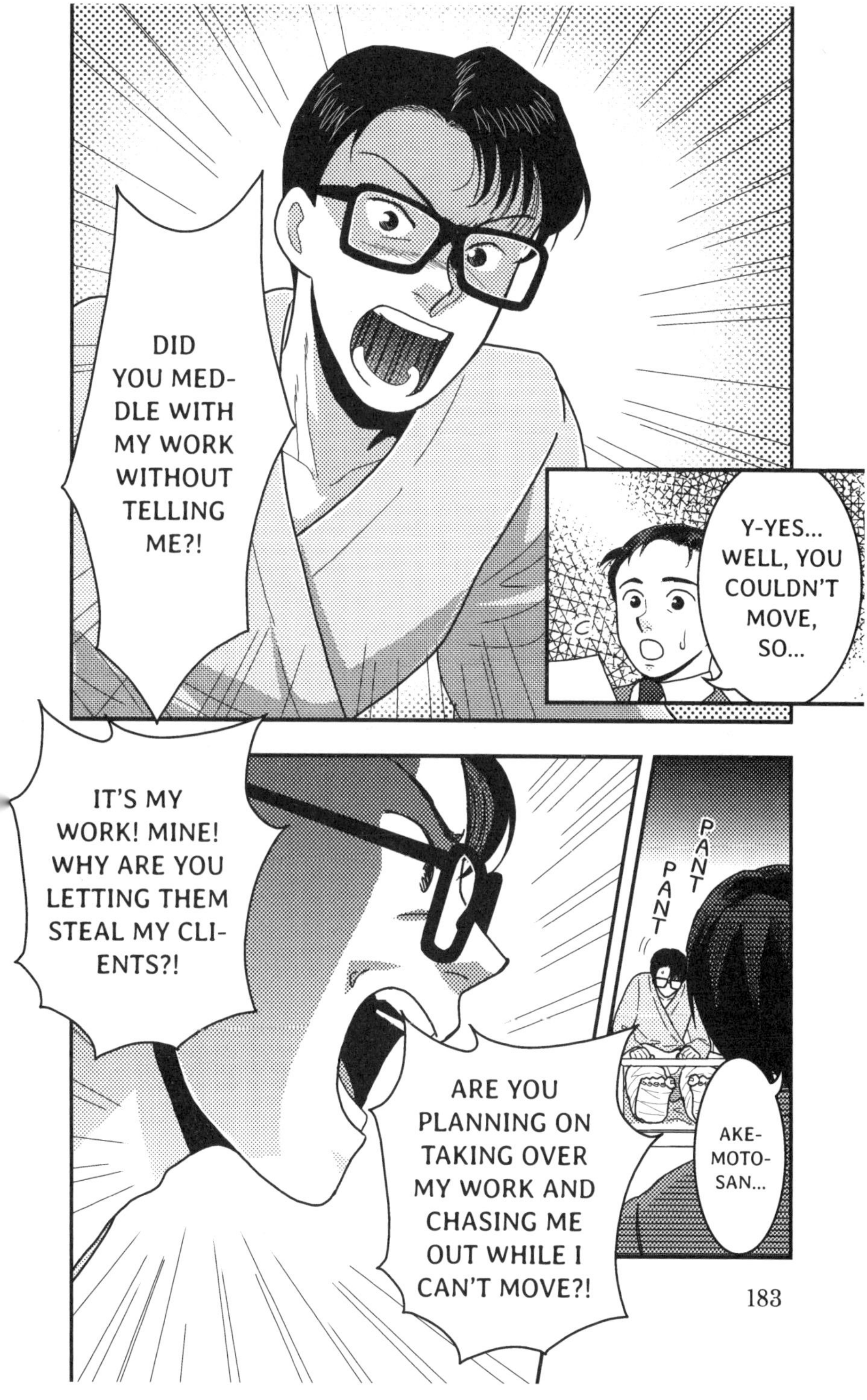
DID YOU MEDDLE WITH MY WORK WITHOUT TELLING ME?!
Y-YES... WELL, YOU COULDN'T MOVE, SO...
IT'S MY WORK! MINE! WHY ARE YOU LETTING THEM STEAL MY CLIENTS?!
PANT PANT
AKE-MOTO-SAN...
ARE YOU PLANNING ON TAKING OVER MY WORK AND CHASING ME OUT WHILE I CAN'T MOVE?!

AKEMO-TO-SAN, YOU'RE VALUABLE BOTH TO ME AND THE STORE.

LIES!

YOU'VE JUST GONE AND CHANGED EVERY-THING AROUND!

OUR BRANCH WAS PER-FORMING JUST FINE!

THAT'S TRUE.

HOWEVER, AS THINGS STAND, SALES WERE BOUND TO DROP.

I'M SURE YOU NOTICED AS WELL, AKEMO-TO-SAN.

THIS IS THE ONLY WAY I CAN WORK.

I DON'T MIX WITH ALL THIS CORE TEAM AND TEAM SALES WHATNOT.

I HEARD THE PRESIDENT OF ITSUKI TAXI GOT VERY ANGRY WHEN HANAMI-KUN WENT TO MEET HIM.

HE INSISTED HE WON'T SIGN THE CONTRACT UNLESS IT'S YOU.

WE EXPLAINED YOUR CIRCUMSTANCES.

HE FINALLY CALMED DOWN AFTER WE PROMISED HIM THAT HE'LL BE ASSIGNED TO YOU ONCE YOU'RE BETTER.

MUTO REAL ESTATE AND KATO TRANSPORT DIDN'T WANT ANYONE ELSE HANDLING THEIR ACCOUNTS EITHER.

YOU'RE HIGHLY APPRECIATED BY YOUR CLIENTS. WHYEVER WOULD YOU THINK THAT WE'D WANT TO GET RID OF YOU?

THE SAME GOES FOR ME AND OTHER EMPLOYEES AT THE STORE.

PLEASE SHARE YOUR TOP SALES TECHNIQUES WITH EVERYONE ELSE.

NGH.

AKEMOTOSAN?

H-HA-HAHA-HA!

YOU'RE SERIOUSLY ASKING ME TO TEACH EVERYONE ABOUT SALES WORK?

YES, I AM.

FINE. IF YOU REALLY WANT ME TO TEACH THEM, THEY CAN GIVE ME THEIR BEST SHOT.

IN EX-CHANGE, I'LL ALSO GIVE EVERY-THING I'VE GOT.

I WON'T STAY QUI-ET LIKE I DID BE-FORE.

THAT'S EXACTLY WHAT I WANT!

A FEW MON- THS AFTER THAT...

...TEAM SALES GOT IMPLE- MENTED IN THE ENTIRE STORE JUST AS AKEMO- TO-SAN RETURNED TO WORK.

THERE WAS UNITY IN THE EN- TIRE SALES DEPART- MENT AND THE AT- MOSPHERE OF THE STORE HAS CHANGED GREATLY.

THANK YOU VERY MUCH!

OH...

...THE STORE AMBIENCE HAS GOT- TEN BETTER, HASN'T IT?

CLICK CLACK

HELLO. THIS IS SAKIGA- KE. OH, MIZUSHI- NA-SAN!

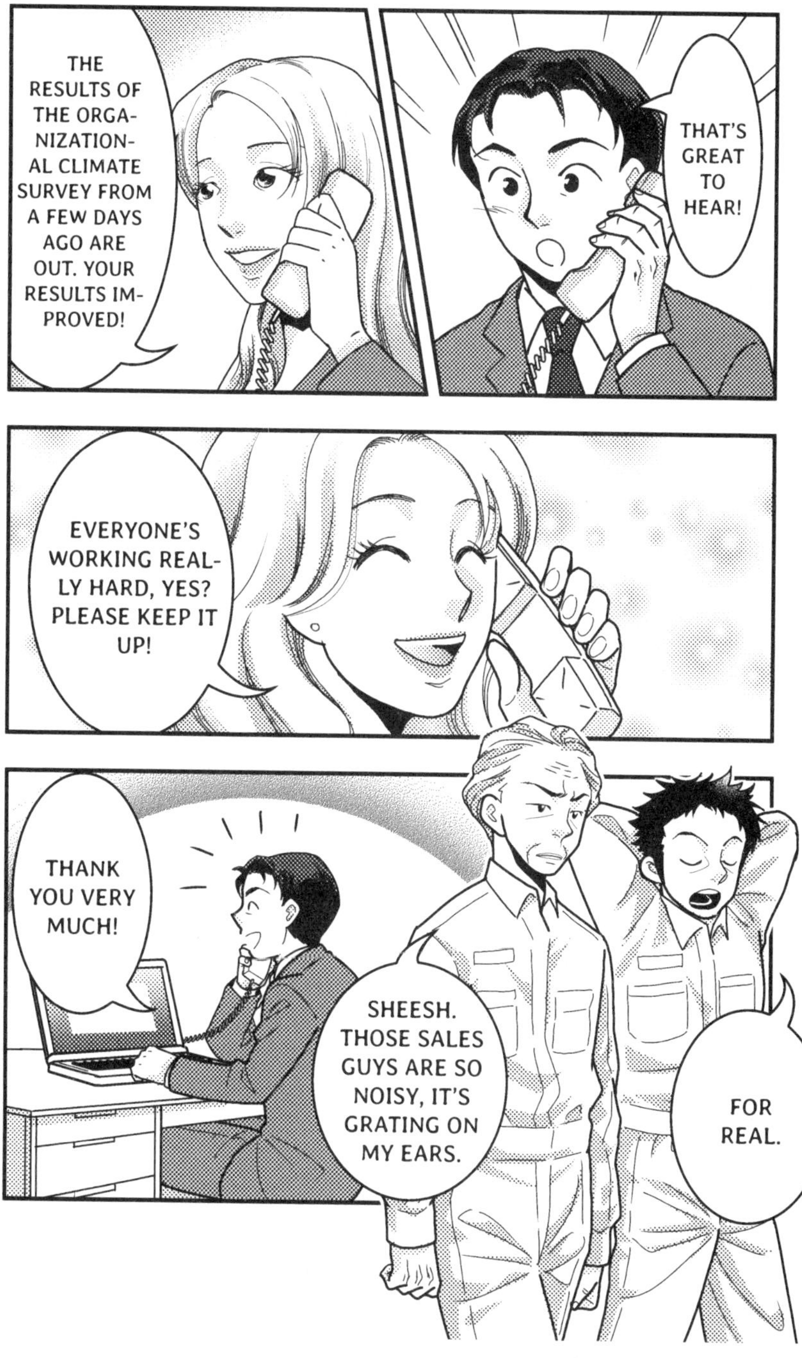
THE RESULTS OF THE ORGA-NIZATION-AL CLIMATE SURVEY FROM A FEW DAYS AGO ARE OUT. YOUR RESULTS IM-PROVED!
THAT'S GREAT TO HEAR!
EVERYONE'S WORKING REAL-LY HARD, YES? PLEASE KEEP IT UP!
THANK YOU VERY MUCH!
SHEESH. THOSE SALES GUYS ARE SO NOISY, IT'S GRATING ON MY EARS.
FOR REAL.

For years, sales manager Akemoto has worked focusing on his individual sales achievements. He's the type of person who follows his superior's orders, so on the surface, he was going along with the store manager's initiatives (driving change through the core team, resumption of the morning meetings, and the introduction of team sales work), but he didn't truly agree with any of them.

Akemoto and Sakigake have different views and values regarding sales work.

Everyone has their own values and views when it comes to work and many other things. When someone joins an organization, they start to slowly absorb the views and values that are dominant in that organization.

In corporations, especially, the majority of people are like Akemoto, whose top priority is focused on his own individual efforts and how to achieve results from them.

This mainstream view disagrees with the views and values of Organization Development, which believes that fostering cooperative relationships can improve results. Because of this difference, time and time again, you will encounter conflict and discord between members in the Organization Development process.

In this section we will use the term "**mindset**" for these views and compare and contrast the view of the majority and the view that Organization Development values.

In the latter part of Story 5, Akemoto and Sakigake—who have very different views and values— are engaged in a serious discussion and are able to begin building a cooperative relationship. In order for Organization Development to keep progressing, it is important for people in the group with different views and values to have a serious discussion to foster trust and cooperation between themselves.

In the following section, we'll take a look at some things to keep in mind when discussing with and building a cooperative relationship with people whose values and views are different from yours.

Let us take a closer look at what kind of discussion was held with Akemoto, who has a different mindset from everyone else.

5-1 Differences in Mindsets

◆ **The Achievement Mindset Dominates Businesses**

Everyone has different ways of viewing or taking things, different thought patterns, convictions, and sense of values. These many facets of one's heart and mind are all connected. For example, how someone views things will affect their thought patterns, and how they view things is in turn influenced by their values and convictions and so on. In this manner, these facets all operate as one whole. For instance, someone who has an optimistic outlook (way of viewing things) tends to respond affirmatively to themselves and others (way of taking things), is future-oriented (thought pattern), and places importance on enjoying things and believing in people (sense of values). In this way, the many facets of one's mind (way of viewing things, thought patterns, convictions, and values) all come in a set. They are all connected with each other and work together as a whole. This is where the term "**mindset**" comes from.

Everyone has different mindsets, but when people are in an organization, **they tend to conform to the mindset of the majority** in that group. They get influenced by the words exchanged and the culture in that organization and slowly end up having the same mindset as the majority.

Different organizations all have different mindsets, but there is a shared mindset among many businesspeople (especially managers) in many companies. This mindset is that **they have to produce the results that their superiors demand and that the way to do this is by distributing the work to each individual. In order to produce said results each individual will have to work hard to meet their work targets.** In this book, this mindset is referred to as the **achievement mindset.** Akemoto in the story possesses the typical achievement mindset.

One's mindset when it comes to work takes shape as one continues to work in an organization. This mindset then becomes the basis when judging things and deciding a course of action. The longer you work, the more this mindset is solidified and the more stable it is. It also becomes a lot harder to change. Also, the more you're surrounded by people with the same mindset, the stronger this mindset becomes. This is why the achievement mindset is the dominant mindset among businesspeople.

Akemoto possesses the typical achievement mindset.

◆ Moving from the Achievement Mindset to the Organization Development Mindset

In comparison, as explained thus far in this book, Organization Development values moving from individual to cooperative work by having people in a group study the situation by holding a discussion and looking at the adaptive challenges on the human side of the organization. The Organization Development approach is to **improve the efficiency and health of the human side of the organization. This leads to members cooperating with each other and learning together as a team, which in turn results in an improvement in performance.** In this book, we refer to this kind of thought pattern and sense of values as the **Organization Development mindset.**

Shown in Figure 5-1 are some of the main points in the achievement mindset and the Organization Development mindset. The achievement mindset, which most businesspeople (especially managers) possess and the Organization Development mindset, which values cooperation, clash with each other.

Neither the achievement mindset nor the Organization Development mindset is absolutely right or better than the other. Insofar as the discussion in this book is concerned, what we can say is that **the Organization Development mindset tends to be effective in dealing with adaptive challenges.**

| Figure 5-1 | The Mainstream Achievement Mindset and the Organization Development Mindset |

The achievement mindset, which is commonplace in the business world	The Organization Development mindset, which values discussion and cooperation
Prioritizes results and achievements	Performance can be improved by fostering cooperative relationships
Focused on short-term results and achievements	Also focuses on the long-term development and growth of the human side of the organization
Optimization and individualizing of work through division of labor	Reform and learning through discussion and cooperation
Proposal and approvement (submit proposal to the manager, manager approves or disapproves)	Discussion and study (study with the manager)
Solves technical problems using existing solutions	Deals with adaptive challenges by having everyone concerned treat it as their own problem and studying, testing, and learning together
Change things	Change ourselves
Management Theory X	Management Theory Y

In the story, Akemoto possesses the achievement mindset while Sakigake (after being influenced and changing through the Organization Development process) possesses the Organization Development mindset. As these two mindsets are contrasting, we keep seeing the differences between these two characters until finally, they clash in Story 5.

In the Organization Development process, there are times when people's mindsets do not agree with one another; thus conflict and discord are born. Figuring out how to discuss and build a cooperative relationship with the people who possess different ways of thinking (achievement mindset) is important to keep the Organization Development process moving.

5-2 Discussion with People You're in Conflict with

◆ The Pattern in Connections That Don't Go Well

In the Organization Development process, you
may encounter a situation where someone with the
Organization Development mindset will need to have a
discussion with someone with the achievement mindset
in order to improve their workplace or organization (just
as the store manager Sakigake and Akemoto had to in
the hospital). Let us look at this discussion through Otto
Scharmer's four-level model, which was earlier introduced
in Part 1.

First, we can see the ① **polite conversation** level in
how Akemoto has interacted with Sakigake until he was
hospitalized. No conflict arises, but they are also unable to
influence each other and cause change. The ② **debate** level
is the kind of exchange we usually have in our everyday
lives with people who have different ways of thinking than
us. At the debate level, people do not try to understand one
another, and no cooperative relationship is born.

◆ Discussing and Building a Cooperative Relationship with People You're in Conflict with

In Story 5, Sakigake attempts to have an ③ **introspective
discussion**. He listens sympathetically to the other party's

story and focuses on the other party's strength. Since Sakigake did not try to insist which mindset was right or wrong, their conversation didn't go down to the ② debate level, and he was able to sympathize with the other party (Akemoto).

In a ④ **productive discussion**, the parties involved look at the situation as a whole and discuss how to realize the common future they're aiming for. They overcome differences in position and mindset, and new ideas and possibilities are born. This is the level where cooperation with a person who has a different mindset becomes possible.

When there is conflict or discord between people with differing mindsets or ways of connecting with others, they will tend to see the problem that's happening between them. However, even if they try to solve this problem, they may end up seeing only their differences, and their discussion won't go well. Just as Sakigake did, in order to build a cooperative relationship with someone you don't agree with, it's important to focus on their strengths. There is an Organization

I'M SURE YOU NOTICED THAT AS WELL, AKEMOTO-SAN.

In the story, Sakigake chose to have an introspective discussion, and this led to their cooperation.

Development approach that focuses on **having a discussion that investigates the strengths and assets of both parties.** This approach is called **appreciative inquiry (AI).**

◆ **Using Appreciative Inquiry (AI) in Discussions**

Appreciative inquiry is an approach that's recently garnering attention in the field of Organization Development. Appreciative means to give value or affirm something, and inquiry means to ask or study something.

According to David Cooperrider, the proponent of this approach, most approaches in Organization Development and transformation tend to narrow their focus to problems and weaknesses (where things don't go well) in order to try to solve them. He then advocated to **focus on the strengths and good features of people and organizations and study how to maximize these strengths** instead of focusing on problems and weaknesses. In AI, you focus on the strengths and assets of people and teams which are already valuable and discuss how to exhibit this value or strength in order to realize the common goal that all parties are aiming for.

YOU'RE HIGHLY APPRECIATED BY YOUR CLIENTS. WHYEVER WOULD YOU THINK THAT WE'D WANT TO GET RID OF YOU?

Sakigake's words for Akemoto make use of appreciative inquiry.

In order to build a cooperative relationship with someone who has a different thought pattern or sense of values, you must leverage the idea of AI and **focus on both your and the other party's strengths and discuss how to achieve the common goal that you're both aiming for.**

This practice of focusing on strengths while maintaining discussion is also important for teams with diverse members in order for people to overcome their differences and cooperate with each other.

When working with team members who think differently or have different values, there are times when things don't progress smoothly. This leads to irritation and conflict, and the difference in thinking and opinions leads to a debate, which makes it harder for the team to move forward. It may be possible to resolve these conflicts, but when there are many differences between people, these conflicts and confrontations tend to resurface after some time. **Constantly trying to solve these problems only consumes energy, and the team doesn't get revitalized or become engaged.**

In AI, people will discuss each member's strengths and potential as well as the strengths of the team as a whole. The differences of the members in a diverse team are not taken as a wall that leads to conflict and disagreement but are instead taken positively as **the members possessing different types of strengths.** Everyone then focuses on each

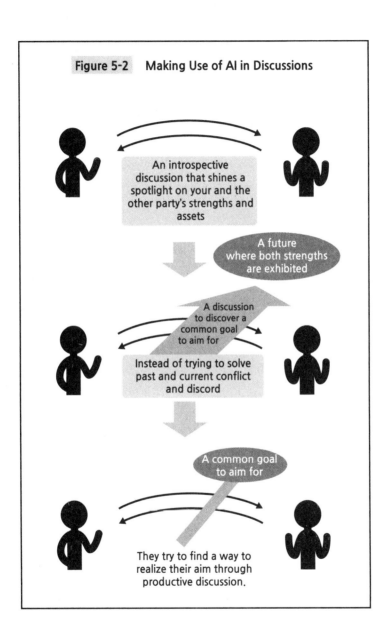

Figure 5-2   Making Use of AI in Discussions

An introspective discussion that shines a spotlight on your and the other party's strengths and assets

A future where both strengths are exhibited

A discussion to discover a common goal to aim for

Instead of trying to solve past and current conflict and discord

A common goal to aim for

They try to find a way to realize their aim through productive discussion.

other's strengths and potential and **looks for possibilities on how to use these strengths to their fullest potential.**

With this approach, the parties concerned can move up from the debate level, where they discuss their differences to find out which is right or wrong, to the introspective discussion level, where they understand each other's strengths and sympathize with each other.

In order to foster cooperation with people you don't agree with, it's important to focus on your strengths and discuss how to realize the common goal you're aiming toward instead of trying to solve disagreements and conflicts.

Part 5

Deepening and Expansion throughout the Organization as a Whole

STORY 6
FROM CONFRONTATION TO COOPERATION

I'D LIKE TO REPLACE MY CAR AC.

BUT SHIBUYA-SAMA, IT'S ONLY BEEN SIX MONTHS SINCE YOU BOUGHT YOUR CAR. IS SOMETHING WRONG WITH THE AC?

NO, IT'S JUST THAT THIS YEAR, MY FAMILY AND I HAVE BEEN SUFFERING FROM HAY FEVER...

...SO I WANTED TO GET ONE THAT COMES WITH AN AIR PURIFYING FUNCTION.

OH, I HOPE YOU AND YOUR FAMILY GET BETTER SOON.

IN THAT CASE...

HM?

LET'S SEE. THIS NEEDS AC REPLACE-MENT—

HEY, TAKA-HASHI!

COME HERE FOR A MIN-UTE!

THIS CAR'S AC IS STILL FINE. IT JUST NEEDS A FILTER CHANGE. WHY REPLACE IT?

BUT...

IT'S FINE. JUST RE-PLACE IT WITH A NEW ONE.

THE CUS-TOMER SAID HE WANTS IT REPLACED, SO LET'S RE-PLACE IT!

ANYWAY, I'M BUSY! I'M GOING BACK TO WORK!

DURING THE REGULAR CORE TEAM MEETING...

THIS ISN'T NEW, BUT IT SEEMS ENGINEERING AND SALES REALLY DON'T GET ALONG.

THAT GOES FOR ALL STORES, THOUGH.

SALES PEOPLE AND ENGINEERS ARE JUST INCOMPATIBLE. OUR ATTITUDES ARE TOO DIFFERENT.

EVEN SO, ENGINEERS ARE ESSENTIAL TO DEALERS.

EXACTLY. RAISING THE STORE SALES COULD BECOME DIFFICULT IF WE DON'T IMPROVE THE RELATIONSHIP BETWEEN ENGINEERS AND SALES.

HOW ABOUT WE TRY ORGANIZATIONAL DIAGNOSTICS?

IN ORDER TO DO THAT...

WHISPER

?

DIAGNOSTICS...

COME TO THINK OF IT, HAVE WE EVER REALLY CONSIDERED WHAT THE ENGINEERS ARE THINKING?

WELL...

UHH...

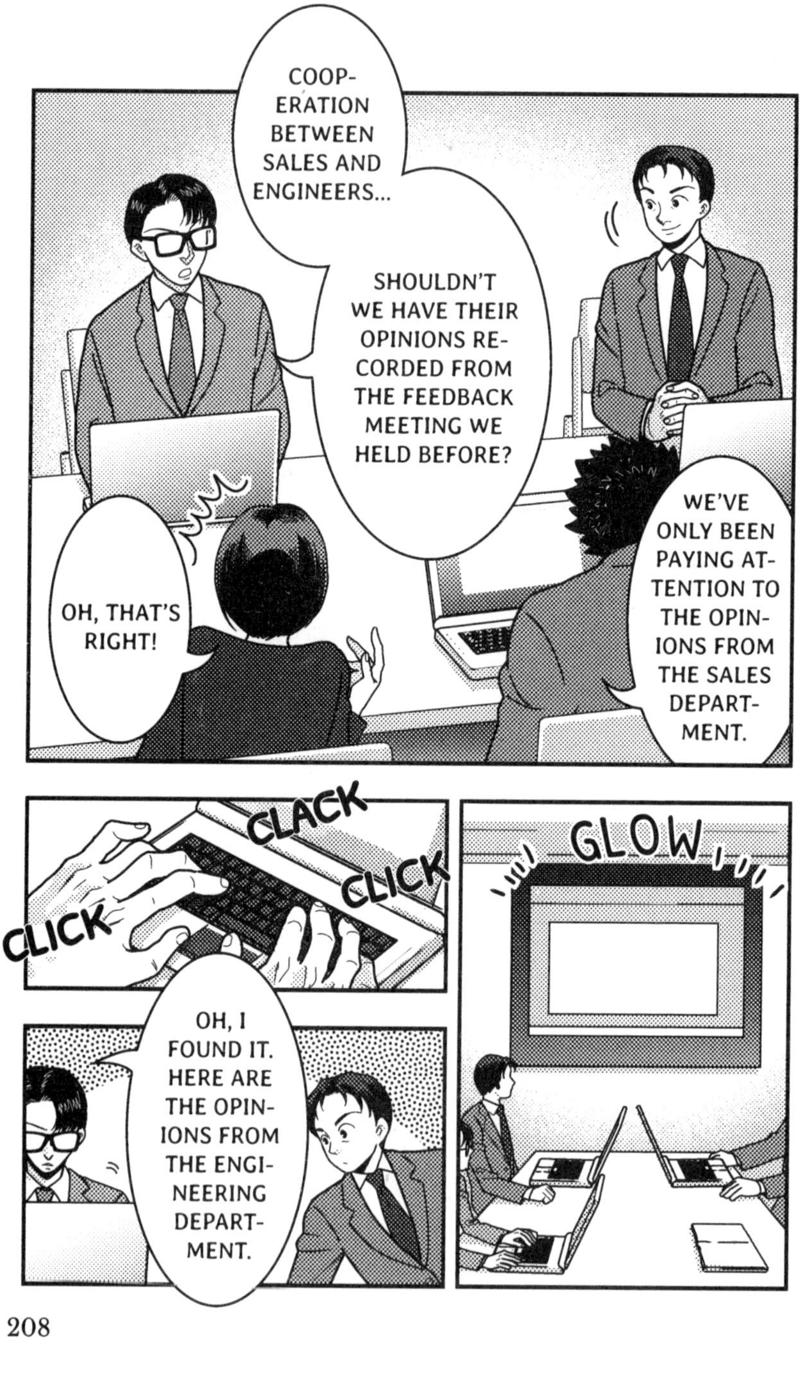
COOP-ERATION BETWEEN SALES AND ENGINEERS...
SHOULDN'T WE HAVE THEIR OPINIONS RE-CORDED FROM THE FEEDBACK MEETING WE HELD BEFORE?
WE'VE ONLY BEEN PAYING AT-TENTION TO THE OPIN-IONS FROM THE SALES DEPART-MENT.
OH, THAT'S RIGHT!
CLACK
CLICK
CLICK
GLOW
OH, I FOUND IT. HERE ARE THE OPIN-IONS FROM THE ENGI-NEERING DEPART-MENT.

OPINIONS FROM THE ENGINEERS

- I GUESS PEOPLE FROM SALES THINK THEY'RE ABOVE US.

- THEY JUST KEEP SAYING IT'S FOR THE CUSTOMER AND THEN PROCEED TO MAKE US MEET UNREASONABLE DEMANDS.

- I WISH THEY'D AT LEAST PREPARE THE SHEET AND MAT WHEN WE'RE DOING AN INSPECTION.

- I CAN FEEL A WALL BETWEEN US AND THE SALES PEOPLE.

NO. IT SHOULDN'T BE TOO LATE TO BRIDGE THE DIVIDE BETWEEN THE TWO DEPARTMENTS.

HOW ABOUT ASKING NIWA-SAN TO JOIN THE CORE TEAM?

BUT WHAT CAN WE DO?

OH! NIWA-SAN'S THE SERVICE MANAGER, SO HE'S PERFECT FOR THE JOB!

HE DOESN'T SEEM LIKE HE'LL JOIN US THOUGH.

210

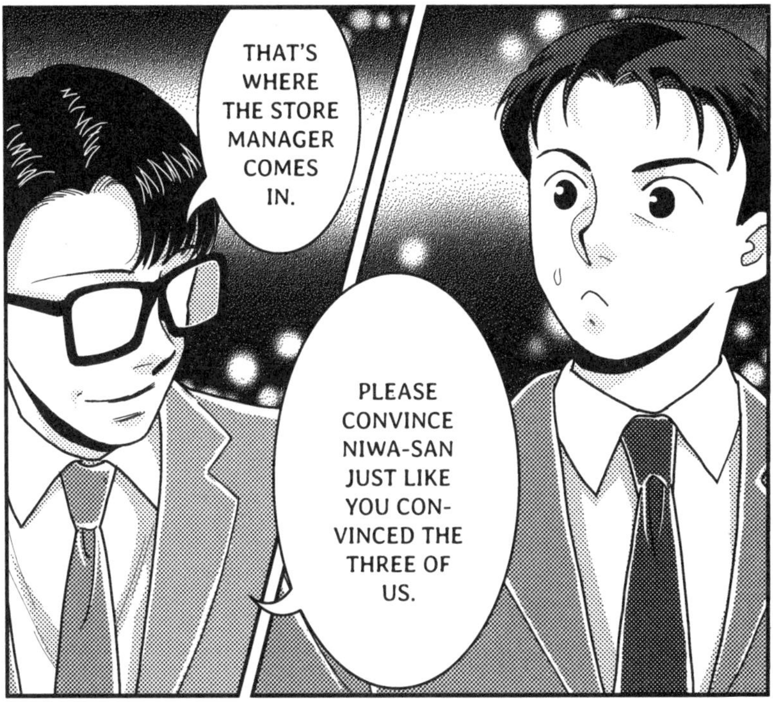
THAT'S WHERE THE STORE MANAGER COMES IN.
PLEASE CONVINCE NIWA-SAN JUST LIKE YOU CONVINCED THE THREE OF US.

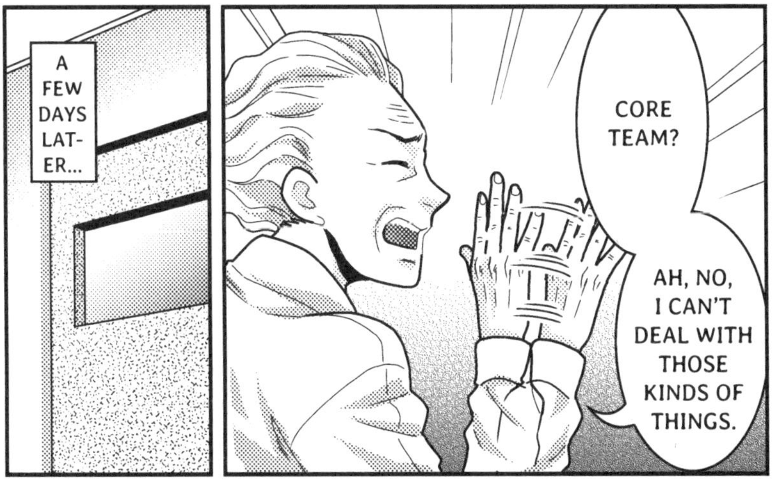
A FEW DAYS LATER...
CORE TEAM?
AH, NO, I CAN'T DEAL WITH THOSE KINDS OF THINGS.

Y'CAN ALL DO THAT BY YOURSELVES, CAN'T YOU?

WELL, WE WANT TO CONSIDER OPINIONS FROM THE ENGINEERING DEPARTMENT AS WELL.

YOU SAY THAT, BUT YOU'LL JUST IGNORE WHAT WE HAVE TO SAY ANYWAY.

THAT MIGHT HAVE BEEN TRUE UP UNTIL NOW...

...BUT THE CORE TEAM EXISTS PRECISELY TO CHANGE THAT.

...

212

SORRY TO SAY, BUT I STILL DON'T TRUST YOU.

...

I UNDERSTAND. FEELINGS DON'T CHANGE THAT EASILY.

AUTHOR PERSONNEL

TRUTH IS, I GOT INVITED TO JOIN THAT CORE TEAM.

WHAT?!

ANOTHER OF THAT STORE MANAGER'S IDEAS, HUH?

THINK YOU'RE BETTER OFF SKIPPING ON THAT ONE, CHIEF.

YEAH, YEAH.

THOSE PEOPLE FROM SALES PROBABLY WON'T EVEN LISTEN TO ANYTHING FROM US ENGINEERS ANYWAY.

I MYSELF THOUGHT THAT WAY AT FIRST.

BUT THE REALITY IS THAT THE STORE DID CHANGE SINCE THAT MANAGER TOOK OVER.

OH YEAH. I KEEP SEEING THE SALES PEOPLE DISCUSSING THINGS TOGETHER LATELY.

SEEMS THEY EXCHANGE INFORMATION ON CLIENTS BEFORE AND AFTER THEIR MEETINGS.

OH?

THEY'VE NEVER DONE THAT BEFORE, RIGHT?

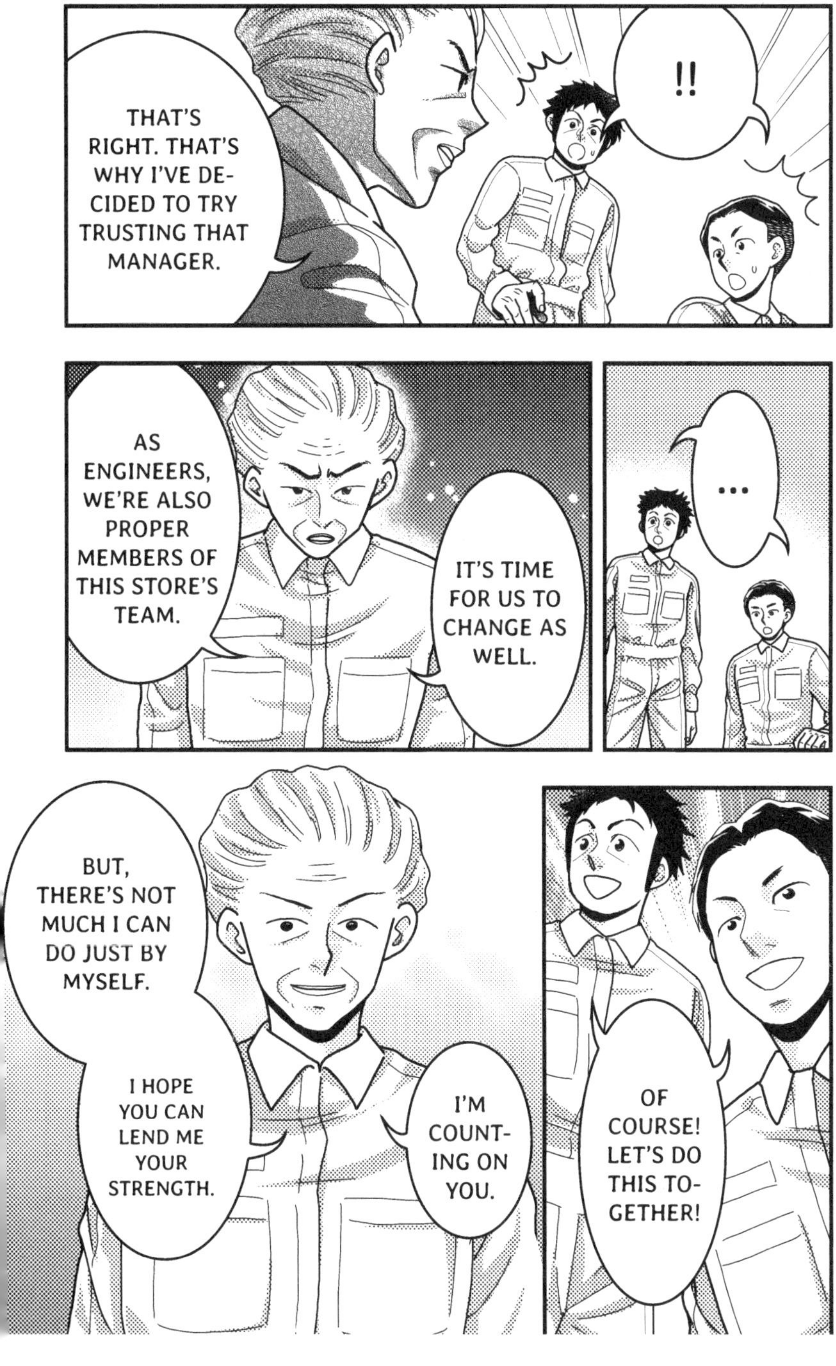
THAT'S RIGHT. THAT'S WHY I'VE DE-CIDED TO TRY TRUSTING THAT MANAGER.
!!
AS ENGINEERS, WE'RE ALSO PROPER MEMBERS OF THIS STORE'S TEAM.
IT'S TIME FOR US TO CHANGE AS WELL.
...
BUT, THERE'S NOT MUCH I CAN DO JUST BY MYSELF.
I HOPE YOU CAN LEND ME YOUR STRENGTH.
I'M COUNT-ING ON YOU.
OF COURSE! LET'S DO THIS TO-GETHER!

THEN, WHAT SHOULD WE DO FIRST?

LET ME THINK. WELL...

FOR EX-AM-PLE...

...

MR. STORE MAN-AGER!

COME OVER HERE A MINUTE. LET'S TALK.

TWITCH

C-COM-ING...

STAFF ONLY

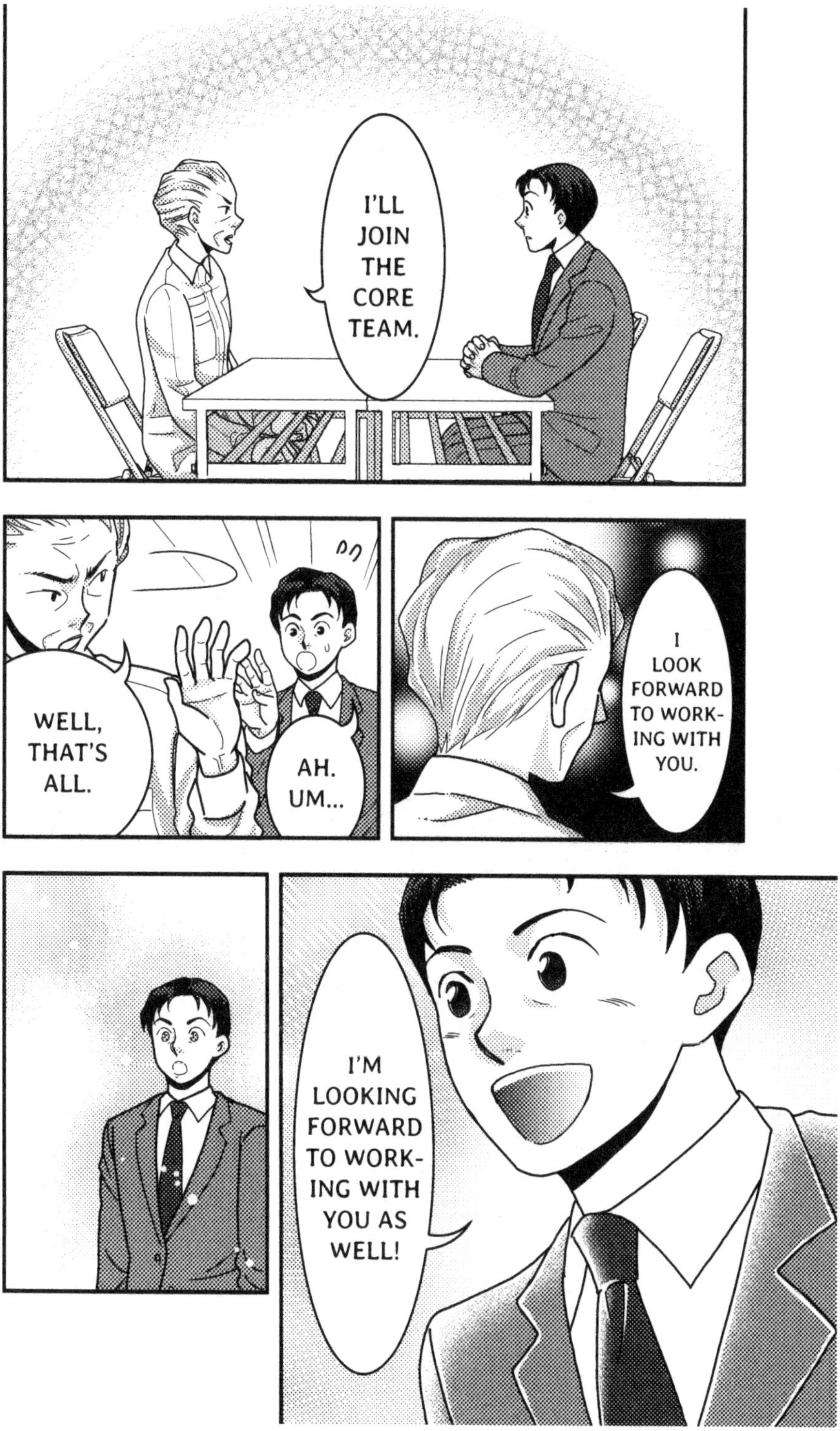
I'LL JOIN THE CORE TEAM.
WELL, THAT'S ALL.
AH. UM...
I LOOK FORWARD TO WORK-ING WITH YOU.
I'M LOOKING FORWARD TO WORK-ING WITH YOU AS WELL!

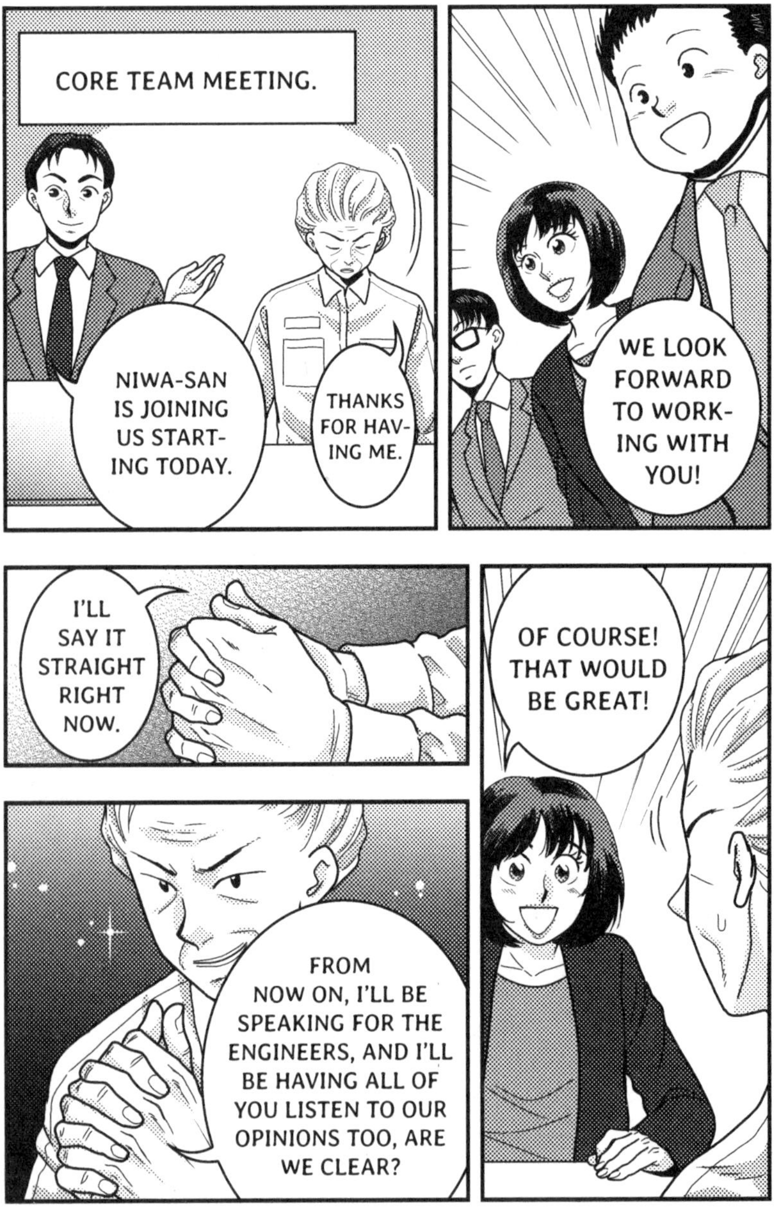
CORE TEAM MEETING.
NIWA-SAN IS JOINING US STARTING TODAY.
THANKS FOR HAVING ME.
WE LOOK FORWARD TO WORKING WITH YOU!
I'LL SAY IT STRAIGHT RIGHT NOW.
FROM NOW ON, I'LL BE SPEAKING FOR THE ENGINEERS, AND I'LL BE HAVING ALL OF YOU LISTEN TO OUR OPINIONS TOO, ARE WE CLEAR?
OF COURSE! THAT WOULD BE GREAT!

OH, RIGHT! PLEASE JOIN US FOR OUR REGULAR SALES MEETINGS AS WELL!

CAN YOU ALSO ACCOMPANY US FOR CLIENT MEETINGS?

IF IT ISN'T TOO MUCH TROUBLE, I'D ALSO LIKE TO OBSERVE THE CAR SERVICING PROCESS.

O-OH! ALL OF THAT SOUNDS GOOD!

AFTER THIS, THE SALES AND ENGINEERING DEPARTMENT CONTINUED THEIR EFFORTS BY THEIR OWN INITIATIVE.

Up until Story 5, Organization Development had only been implemented within the sales department. After this effort showed results, the core team widened their focus to include the entirety of the store. They started to work on the constantly problematic relationship between the sales and engineering department.

Conflict and confrontation between groups, departments, and divisions can be found in various organizations. In this part, we'll be looking at why there is conflict and confrontation between groups in a company and explain the mindset you need to have in dealing with them.

In the final part of the story, the atmosphere in the store had changed with the help of Organization Development. The big changes include how the employees now think things through together through discussions, suggest ideas, and implement these ideas themselves. This state is called self-organization. We'll also be taking a look at the mentality associated with self-organization and the deepening and expansion of Organization Development within a company.

6-1 Implementing Cooperation within a Group

◆ How Conflicts and Confrontation Are Born in a Group

Cooperation and communication between departments or divisions can be quite a difficult topic. In most organizations, there is a wall between different departments and divisions, and more often than not they do not share information and cooperate.

An even more difficult situation is when certain departments or divisions get along badly. In the story of this book, there was a conflict between the engineers and the sales personnel. You will often hear about conflicts and confrontations between different groups in a company like between the sales and development departments, between divisions in the development department, or between HR and field personnel.

There are cases when conflict between groups is caused by actual communication or action, but there are also cases when it's caused by perceptions based on speculation and assumption.

For example, in this book's story, one of the opinions in the hearing results was that there are engineers who felt like sales personnel were looking down on them.

It's likely that this feeling was caused by something that a sales employee did (like cutting an engineer off, saying they're busy). However, on top of this initial encounter, there is also the matter of **how this encounter is interpreted, perceived, and talked about between the engineers.** Speculations and assumptions that an engineer comes up with may influence the situation and worsen their relationship with sales.

For example, engineers may talk among themselves about how the people from sales are always so quick to say that they're busy and assume that sales personnel think that engineers aren't busy. In another conversation, an engineer might share that the people from sales never listen to him and comment that sales personnel probably look down on engineers and think of them as servants. Setting aside whether these assumptions are true or not, this makes them view the situation in a worse light, and they become convinced that this is reality.

Groups tend to perceive their own as more likable and tend to see other groups as worse and be prejudiced against them. This phenomenon is studied in psychology and is known as **in-group bias.** This means that humans have a tendency to perceive a confrontation between them and others to be worse than it actually is, and their speculations and assumptions about other groups tend toward a negative direction.

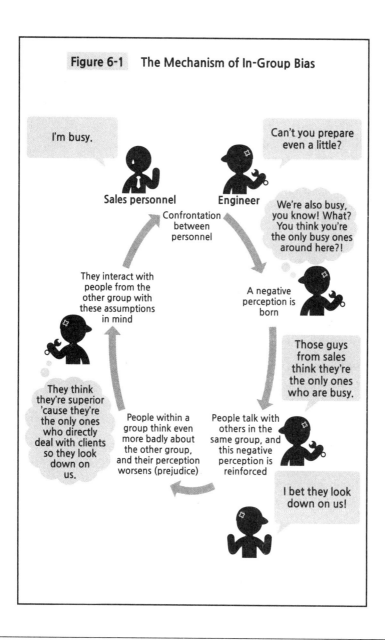

Figure 6-1   The Mechanism of In-Group Bias

Since there is a possibility of the relationship between groups worsening on its own like this, there is a need to deliberately approach the situation and make an effort to build a cooperative relationship between the two.

◆ The Mindset Needed in Building Cooperative Relationships within a Group

Discussion is still the key in repairing a relationship between two groups and attempting to build cooperation between them. By gathering the two groups in one place and discussing how the members feel toward each other and how they perceive their interactions, it becomes possible for the members to correct their own speculations and assumptions.

For instance, the engineers can express that they feel like the people from sales look down on them. They can then have a discussion where the sales personnel can talk about whether this is true or not, and the engineers can share what made them feel this way (**seeing the problem**). Through a discussion like this the sales people might realize how their actions affect the engineers, and the engineers might realize that they've been making assumptions and interpreting their interactions to be worse than they actually are (**serious discussion**).

At this stage, there is a need to engage in introspective discussion where the two groups will stop thinking

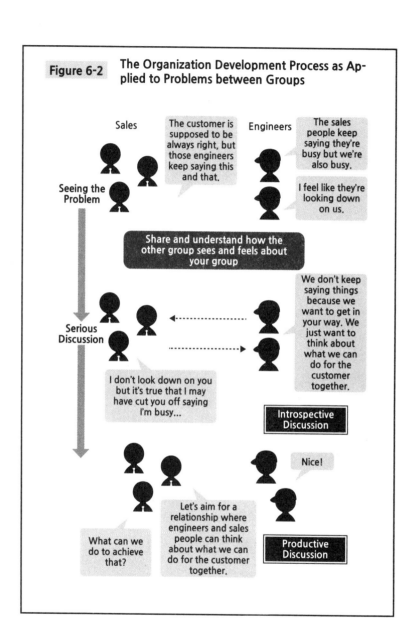

Figure 6-2 The Organization Development Process as Applied to Problems between Groups

that their group's views and feelings are correct and sympathetically listen to each other's views and feelings. Through discussion, the two groups can realize what exactly happened between them. By planning what kind of relationship both parties want to aim for and how to go about achieving this in order to better cooperate with one another, building cooperative relationships between groups becomes possible.

The process is basically the same. The three steps—seeing the problem, serious discussion, and building a future—are applied to the problem between the two groups.

If a core team was established to drive the progress of Organization Development, it can also be effective to have members from both parties in order to build a cooperative relationship between the two groups.

6-2 The Growth and Development of an Organization or Workplace

◆ What Is Self-organization?

By the final part of Story 6, the entire store had already been revitalized. All the employees are thinking about the branch. They suggest ideas (looking at the inspection procedure and engineers accompanying sales personnel in their meetings) and implement new plans on their own (see Figure 6-3).

Organization Development aims to help the human side of organizations and workplaces function well and improve cooperative relationships. At the same time, it also aims to have the organization members move independently and by their own initiative, and if needed, change the hard side of their organization or workplace by themselves. At this stage, the employees don't need to be ordered by their superior. By their own initiative, the members related to the issue will hold a discussion (productive discussion level) to think through things and implement their plans in order to improve the situation all on their own. This is called **self-organization.**

Self-organization is a term in the field of complex systems that refers to the phenomenon by which **various components in a bundle interact and spontaneously form a pattern.** In the context of teams and organizations, this is when various members interact and through discussion, spontaneously cooperate and come up with plans and projects and implement these on their own.

When an organization has become self-organizing, the manager doesn't need to give orders or approval and relinquishes control over what will be done. However, this doesn't mean that the manager abandons their responsibilities and does nothing. The crucial role of the manager is to **endorse and watch over the various independent projects and provide support for these if needed.** The manager will also have to **initiate discussions with members and learn with everyone by going through the three steps of Organization Development.**

◆ Deepening Organization Development and the Growth and Development of an Organization or Workplace

Let us look back at the Organization Development process of the branch in our story.

The Organization Development process of this store began with the hearing and feedback meeting.

Figure 6-3 A Self-organizing Workplace or Organization

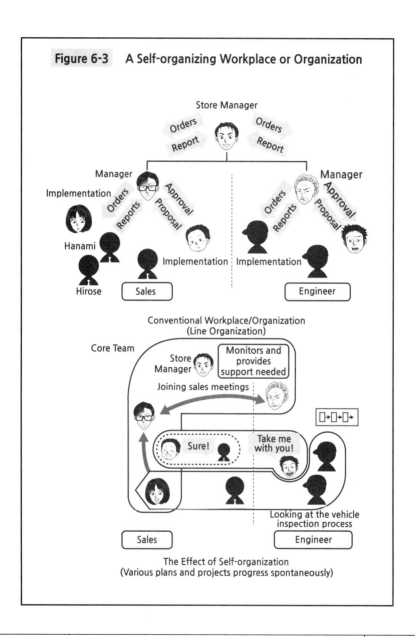

Conventional Workplace/Organization
(Line Organization)

The Effect of Self-organization
(Various plans and projects progress spontaneously)

The process began with organizational diagnostics where a hearing and a feedback meeting was held regarding the current situation in their store (Story 2). After this, the core team was established (Story 3) and they decided to bring back the morning meetings in their aim to build work relationships where everyone can teach one another.

The Organization Development process of this store began with the hearing and feedback meeting (Story 4). This led to the sharing of sales tips and experiences in the morning meetings and the introduction of team sales work. Through this, the skills and abilities of the employees improved as a whole and their workplace changed into a branch that's able to do effective sales work. They were also able to transform the store's competitive relationships into mutually supportive relationships. This is **the period where the effectiveness and health of the organization improved.**

Furthermore, like the visualization of the inspection procedure, the team also decided to review factors on the hard side such as their work procedures. At this stage, the team is changing portions of the hard side of the organization that they can change themselves. This means that their ability to self-innovate has improved. Finally, at the end of Story 6 and in the Epilogue following this section, we can see that the organization has reached a state where various plans are being executed on their own. This is self-organization at work. At the time of Story 2, back when Sakigake began the process of Organization Development with support from Mizushina, he probably didn't realize that the branch would reach this kind of self-organization. Just as this example, a workplace or organization's growth and development progresses with the evolution of their Organization Development process.

The mechanism (unconfirmed) for this is shown in Figure 6-4. **① The stage where Organization Development was started, ② the stage where something isn't functioning properly, ③ the stage where effectiveness and health of the human side of the organization steadily improves, ④ the stage where self-innovation increases and members try to change even the hard side of the organization by themselves, and ⑤ the stage of self-organization.**

In Figure 6-4, the corresponding four levels of discussion as defined by Otto Scharmer et al. are shown at the bottom (this is also unconfirmed). It can be seen in Figure 6-4 that as Organization Development progresses, the discussion level also evolves. There are overall more introspective discussions and productive discussions.

AFTER THIS, THE SALES AND ENGINEERING DEPARTMENT CONTINUED THEIR EFFORTS BY THEIR OWN INITIATIVE.

At the end of Story 6, we can see that the store had reached the state of self-organization.

On the other hand, a certain amount of debate is needed whenever a decision needs to be made. Stage ③, where the effectiveness and health of the organization improves, is located at the center, but this doesn't necessarily mean that it's the halfway point. Reaching stage ③ is a very remarkable

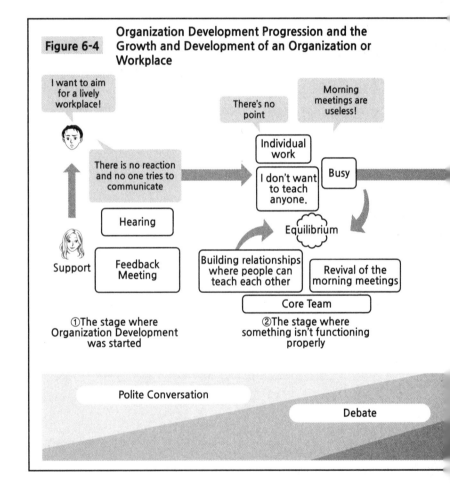

Figure 6-4 Organization Development Progression and the Growth and Development of an Organization or Workplace

progress and it means that the team's Organization Development efforts have produced significant results. Please use this figure as a measure to decide what stage you will be aiming for with your Organization Development efforts.

In Organization Development, **you don't suddenly implement**

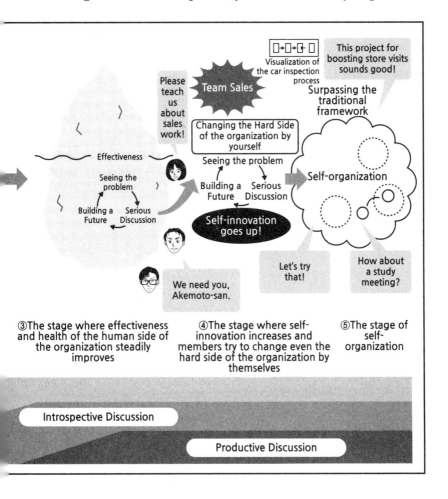

big plans and changes. The point is to **start with small steps in small places.** You need to start with a small scope (like a close team or workplace) and aim to improve their effectiveness and health in response to the current problem. By **repeating small cycles of the steps seeing the problem, serious discussion, and building a future,** the team, workplace, or organization will steadily grow and develop.

◆ Constant Discussion and Pursuit

There is no end in the Organization Development Process. The essence of Organization Development is in **repeating small cycles of seeing the problem, serious discussion, and building a future on a daily basis and holding constant discussions and investigations to deal with problems on the human side of an organization or workplace.**

Organization Development never ends because we **constantly have new adaptive challenges to deal with** (it's common for the problem to go unnoticed, however). When a new member joins a team, when roles change, when new structures or systems are introduced, or when you're faced with a new task at work—any new thing can affect the human side of an organization or workplace. For instance, when a new member joins the team, people will tend to worry whether or not they can adapt to this new workplace. However, at the same time, considering this on the workplace level, welcoming, discussing with, and cooperating with the new member is an adaptive challenge for everyone in the workplace. By going through small steps of seeing the problem, serious discussion, and building a future to deal with this human-side problem of welcoming a new member, it becomes possible to build a more cooperative relationship with this new member as a team. Discussions and investigations about a workplace or team's situation aren't only needed when there is a new member or when structures and systems are changed. When you keep repeating the same things, people will get used to it and this way of perceiving things, thinking through things, and taking action becomes ingrained in everyone. This makes it more difficult for new ideas to be born, decreases discussions between people, and makes learning more difficult as well. That is why there is also a need to discuss and study things when you've gotten used to repeating the same things.

Even if you reach stage ⑤, self-organization (Figure 6-4), that doesn't mean you've reached the end of Organization Development. **By continuously putting in effort to maintain self-organization, the organization can continuously stay in a self-organizing state.** These efforts fundamentally consist of cycling through the three steps of Organization Development and continuously having discussions and studying things.

Constantly having discussions and investigations among the members of an organization or workplace can be likened to watering its rich human side (mutual trust and cooperative relationships) every day and continuously cultivating it.

EPILOGUE

What Does It Mean for an Organization to Change?

WE'RE STARTING THE MEETING!

THE CLIENT WE'RE MEETING TODAY IS...

BEFORE...

HOW ABOUT DOING THIS TODAY?

EVER SINCE NIWA-SAN JOINED THE CORE TEAM, THE ENGINEERS AND SALES PERSONNEL HAVE BEEN WORKING TOGETHER AS A TEAM.

WE'RE GOING OUT TO MEET A CLIENT!

EVERYONE WAS KIND OF AWKWARD AT FIRST, BUT THEY GOT USED TO EACH OTHER IN TIME.

AND NOW...

236

TAIGA MOTOR COMPANY HEAD OFFICE.

SAKIGA-KE-SAN! IT'S BEEN A WHILE.

IT'S NICE TO SEE YOU AGAIN.

I HEARD THREE MONTHS AGO THAT THE ENGINEERING AND SALES DEPART-MENTS LEARNED HOW TO COOPER-ATE WITH EACH OTHER.

YES. IT'S ALL THANKS TO NI-WA-SAN JOINING THE CORE TEAM.

NOWADAYS, ENGINEERS ALSO JOIN THE SALES MEET-INGS WHERE THEY SHARE INFORMATION ABOUT THE CLI-ENTS.

THEY ALSO SOME-TIMES JOIN THE CLIENT MEETINGS.

THE ENTIRE STORE IS NOW WORKING TO-GETHER AS A TEAM.

THE STAFF ALSO COME UP WITH NEW PROJECTS BY THEM-SELVES.

THERE HAVE BEEN ZERO LEAVES AND RESIGNATIONS IN THE PAST FEW MONTHS, AND OUR PERFORMANCE HAS ALSO RISEN.

EVERY-THING SOUNDS GREAT!

THINKING BACK, YOU WERE ALWAYS THERE TO SYM-PATHIZE WITH ME.

IT'S ALL THANKS TO YOU. I NEVER THOUGHT THE EMPLOYEES AND THE ENTIRE STORE COULD CHANGE THIS MUCH.

YOU SOMETIMES GAVE ME THE PUSH I NEED-ED WHILE AT OTHER TIMES OPPOSING ME.

YOU'VE BEEN A VERY REAS-SURING AND RELIABLE FACILITA-TOR.

I TOLD YOU BEFORE THAT YOU DIDN'T UNDERSTAND PEOPLE'S HEARTS, DIDN'T I?

YES! THAT WAS A SHOCK, TO BE HONEST.

HOWEVER, NOW, EVERYONE AND THE WHOLE STORE HAS CHANGED.

THIS REALITY IS PROOF THAT YOU NOW UNDERSTAND PEOPLE'S HEARTS, SAKIGAKE-SAN.

I CAN NOW SAY THIS WITHOUT HESITATION.

OUR WORKPLACE CANNOT CHANGE IF WE DON'T PUT IN THE EFFORT TO CHANGE IT OURSELVES.

NOW THAT YOU UNDERSTAND THAT...

...YOU'LL BE ABLE TO OVERCOME ANY CHALLENGE THAT MAY COME IN THE FUTURE.

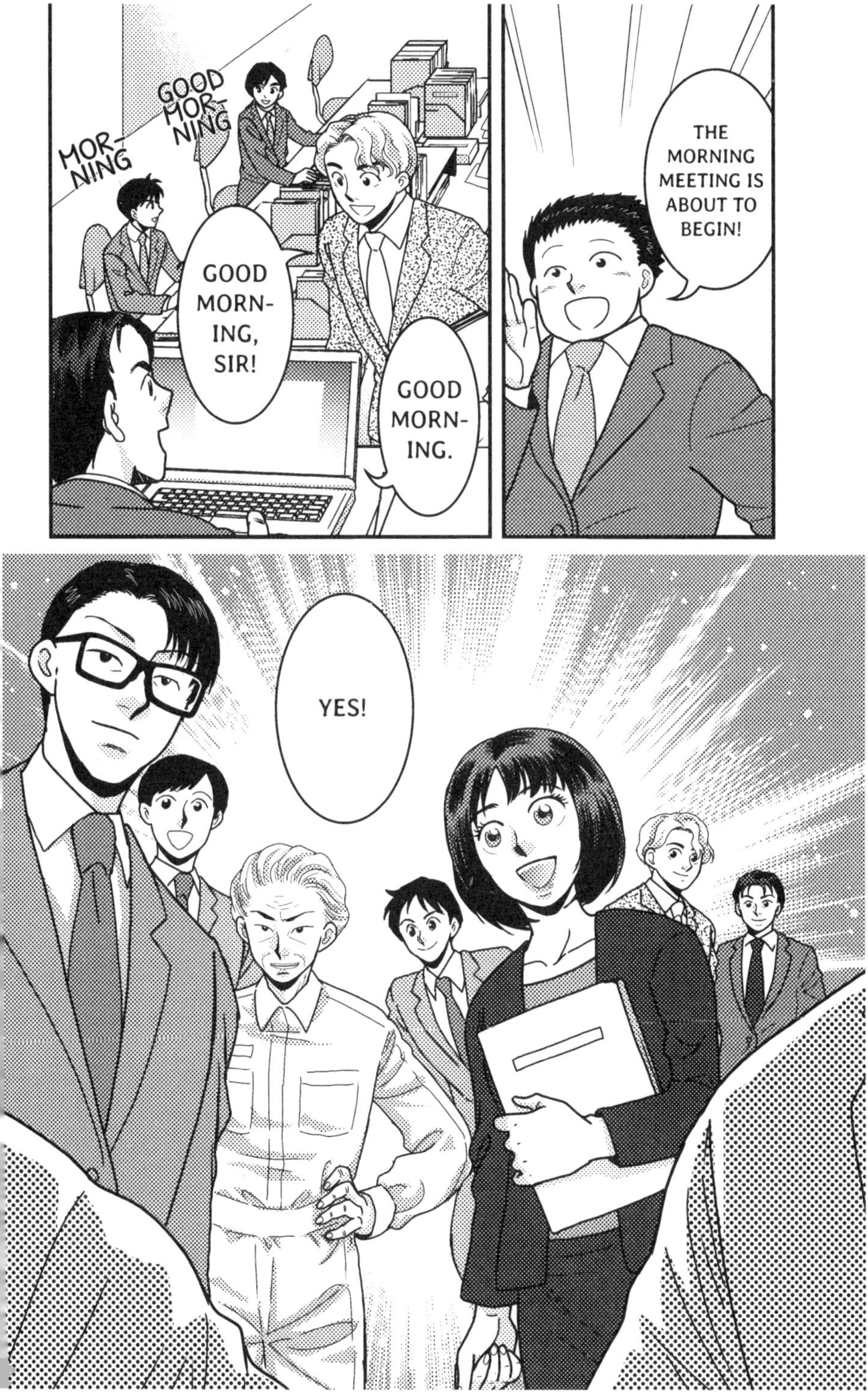
MOR-NING
GOOD MOR-NING
GOOD MORN-ING, SIR!
GOOD MORN-ING.
THE MORNING MEETING IS ABOUT TO BEGIN!
YES!

Afterword

I believe that there are three core components needed in the implementation of Organization Development: ① a mindset or attitude that will become the trunk of your Organization Development, ② a concrete understanding of Organization Development methods and practical skills to implement them, and ③ the ability to recognize and respond to the problems that happen on the human side of organizations and workplaces.

In this book, for the ① mindset or attitude that will become the trunk of your Organization Development, we focused on the key concepts of **discussion** and **cooperation**. I feel that books in the "Manga Guide to..." Series are often written to focus on a certain theory or method. In contrast, this book gathers various theories and methods and deals with the mindsets and attitudes that are valued under the Organization Development umbrella. In that sense, I believe it's a unique book in the series.

In this book, I organized and penned the story with the hope that it will be read by managers (people in charge, assistant managers, section managers, and department heads) and people who want to aid the progress of Organization Development in their own workplace (people from a division's HR department or people who want to implement Organization Development) in particular.

If by reading this book, people can have a clearer image of how people and organizations change through Organization Development and if they can feel more familiar with Organization Development than they did before, then I would be happy to know that this book achieved its aim.

On the other hand, in order for managers and members of a workplace to implement Organization Development, they will need the above-mentioned ② concrete understanding of methods and practical skills to implement them and ③ ability to recognize and respond to the problems. The ③ ability to recognize and respond to the problems, in particular, can only be improved through practice and learning through experience. I hope that the readers who develop an interest in Organization Development through this book (especially managers and working people) choose to learn more about Organization Development by joining a workshop or training, learn various methods there, and improve their abilities through actual experience.

Last but not the least, I would like to extend my heartfelt gratitude to Satomi Kawashibara-san for editing this book, Yoko Matsuo-san for drawing the wonderful manga, Masako Urata-san for her help in the creation of the story and manga, and Jun Okuhira-san for lending me wisdom when I was composing the story in this book.

References

- David Bohm. (2007). *On Dialogue: From Confrontation to Coexistence, From Argument to Discussion.* Eiji Press.
- Gervase Bushe, Robert Marshak (Editors). (2018). *Dialogic Organization Development: Theory and Practice.* Eiji Press.
- Kenneth Gergen, Lone Hersted. (2015). *Dialogue Management: Strong Organization Born from Dialogue.* Discover 21, Inc.
- Lisa Haneberg. (2012). *Organization Development Basics: A Systematic Guide on Basic Theory and Practice for Transforming an Organization.* Human Value.
- Ronald Heifetz. (1996). *What Is Leadership?* Sanno University Publications Department.
- Ronald Heifetz, Marty Linsky. (2018). *Leadership on the Line: Staying Alive through the Dangers of Leading.* Eiji Press.
- Ronald Heifetz, Marty Linsky, Alexander Grashow. (2017). *The Most Difficult Leadership: The Will and Skills for Accomplishing Change.* Eiji Press.
- Adam Kahane. (2008). *Solving Tough Problems through Discussion: How a Facilitator Resolved Apartheid.* Human Value.
- Masanori Kato. (2017). *Can Organizations Change?: Organization Development That Starts from the Top.* Eiji Press.

- Ryo Nakadoi. (2015). *Theory U Made Easy with Manga.* JMA Management Center Inc.
- Jun Nakahara, Kazuhiko Nakamura. (2018). *Inquiring Organization Development.* Diamond, Inc.
- Kazuhiko Nakamura. (2015). *An Introduction to Organization Development: Creating a Lively Workplace.* Kobunsha.
- Richiro Oda. (2017). *Learning Organizations Made Easy with Manga.* JMA Management Center Inc.
- Richiro Oda. (2017). *An Introduction to Learning Organizations.* Eiji Press.
- Edgar Schein. (2012). *Process Consultation Revisited: Building the Helping Relationship.* Hakuto-Shobo Publishing Company.
- Edgar Schein. (2009). *What It Means to Help People: Seven Principles for Building a True Cooperative Relationship.* Eiji Press.

About the Author
Kazuhiko Nakamura

Kazuhiko Nakamura is a professor of human psychology in the Humanities Department and the head of the Human Relations Research Center at Nanzan University.

His areas of expertise include Organization Development, Human Relation Training (Hands-on Laboratory Training), and Group Dynamics. He is a member of the NTL Institute in America and completed their certificate program for Organization Development.

He has experience in providing support in various places as through Organization Development practitioner training and consultation. At the same time, he also engages in action research, which aims to link research and actual practice.

His published works include *An Introduction to Organization Development* (Kobunsha) and *Inquiring Organization Development* (co-author, Diamond, Inc.). He was also the translator for *Dialogic Organization Development: Theory and Practice* (Eiji Press).